AT
ANOTHER
TIME

Growing up in Butte

PAUL B. LOWNEY

AT ANOTHER TIME – GROWING UP IN BUTTE

Copyright 2000, Paul B. Lowney, Seattle, Washington

Second printing, 2000

Third printing, expanded, 2001

ISBN 0-9609946-6-1

CROWNE & LURIE PUBLISHERS, SEATTLE, WASHINGTON

Acknowledgments

For assistance in preparing this book for publication, my thanks to Lisa McCoy, Velvet Hansen, Harry Pruzan, Lori Reinhall, Larry Buckley, William Hardy, Kjersty Stone, the Butte High School Library, the Butte-Silver Bow Public Library, and the World Museum of Mining in Butte.

Design & typography by Spencer Rossman

My gratitude to my philosophy professors for stimulating my thinking and my writings with teachings in logic, metaphysics, and dialectics, and for encouraging me to doubt and then to reason on the doubt: Professors Edwin Marvin, University of Montana; Arthur Smullyan and Melvin Rader, University of Washington.

Other books by Paul Lowney: (hardbacks) Offbeat Humor, The Best in Offbeat Humor, The Best in Offbeat Humor II, The Love Game, Gleeb, The Big Book of Gleeb, Toads, No Charge for Dreaming; (paperbacks) This is Hydroplaning, Seattle – the Nation's Most Beautiful City, Washington – America's Most Scenic State, The Best of Gleeb, The Pocket Gleeb, Toads, Little Lessons From Life, My Professors & My Jewish Mother, Ergo 1.

Contents

A note to the reader

In a book I wrote a few years ago titled *The Best in Offbeat Humor II*, I included a section of stories about growing up in Butte, Montana. Many people commenting on the book praised these stories, and some readers said, "Why don't you do a whole book of them?" I agreed. It took me a year as a spare-time project, but eventually I put together this volume.

The book is not intended to be a documentary history of Butte and its culture in those past years, but rather, based mostly on vivid memories, it is a recitation of little episodes and commentaries about Butte and my early life in this small, immigrant-diverse, copper-mining town nestled along the west side of the Continental Divide.

Primarily, I did this book for myself and my many relatives and friends to preserve these thoughts and events from a bygone time so that they would not be lost in the passage of years. It is serendipity if others find interest in these pages.

Much in the following text is about the Lowney family: myself, my three siblings, Lee, Sam, and Hank; and my Jewish mother and father, Bessie and Mark, who were born in Lithuania, met and married in Glasgow, Scotland, and entered this country many years ago through Ellis Island, New York. (And let's not forget, there is a piece in this book about my wonderful dog, Freddy, for whom I had great affection.)

My father's real name was Lurie, as are the names of my relatives in Scotland and California. According to my father, the name Lurie was accidentally changed to Lowney in the records at Ellis Island, and my father didn't seem to care one way or the other about this mistake, because he was beginning a new life in a new land.

There was nothing particularly outstanding about my life in Butte, but mostly it was a happy, busy, and eventful time. Maybe this was because I was young, blessed with good looks, was eager and ambitious, and I could feel both the joy and the pain to the fullest measure.

What amazes me in a backward view, is the almost photographic recall of events and conversations locked into my memories, perhaps because my young brain had plenty of storage space and an abundance of the strong alpha brain waves that are effective in imprinting mental impressions.

Let's hope, that through a small window to this past, these stories engender some pleasant feelings and thoughtfulness, and that they bring to life many delightful scenes from a bygone time.

PAUL B. LOWNEY

Seattle, 2000

Dedicated to my parents
Mark and Bessie
who
In their brief lives
Gave so much.

All my past life is mine no more;
The flying hours are gone,
Like transitory dreams given o'er
Whose images are kept in store
By memory alone.

– John Wilmot (1647-1680)

The Lowney Family
in Butte, Montana

Father

MARK

Mother

BESSIE

Sister

LEE

Brother

SAM

Brother

HANK

PAUL

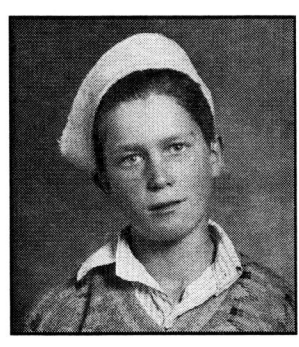

A byline and my mother

I burst into the house after school and said: "Look, Ma, my name is in the Butte High School paper, *The Mountaineer*. It's my first byline."

My mother looked at me unimpressed, shrugged her shoulders, and said: "*Nu*, did you get money for it?"

"It's not the money," I said in exasperation. "It's the recognition. I want to be a writer and now I have my name in print. Everything isn't money. You're from the Old Country and you just don't understand."

Thinking back about that conversation, I realize that my mother had a point. Not that you should get paid for writing in a school paper, but the general concept. Getting paid makes you a professional. The world is full of unpaid writers, probably because at one time or another we all yearn to set down our experiences and our innermost thoughts – and writing is inexpensive and an easy art form. No fancy equipment required – only a pen and a piece of paper. But make no mistake about it, good writing is a painstaking craft that embraces two concepts: 1. The content of what you have to say and 2. The craftsmanship of how you say it. Craftsmanship without content won't go very far. Content without craftsmanship has a better chance.

In its elemental form, writing is simply the process of using words as symbols to transfer images and ideas from the writer's mind to the reader's (or listener's) mind – and for my style, as simply and clearly as possible without the clutter of verbiage.

My mother died young, but she did live long enough to see my first money for writing – a small check for first prize in a national letter-writing contest for youths, sponsored by *King Features Syndicate*. But my writing, and also my publishing, hadn't brought in any big money. Years later it did. I wish I could tell my mother: "Look, Ma, you were right. I now get paid for my writing. See how well-off I am. I can do so much for you." It pains me that she doesn't know this – unless, of course, if in some mysterious veiled beyond, she knows.

My mother – the poker player

During a miners' strike, there were hard economic times in Butte, and my father's small plumbing business did poorly. My father was always concerned about stretching our money, so when my mother would come home from one of her ladies' poker parties, he would ask, "Did you win or lose?" If my mother won, she would proudly announce that she had won and tell the exact amount. If she lost, she would say to my father, "I didn't win. I didn't lose; I broke out even." I can't remember my mother ever saying she lost. She either won or she broke out even. Finally I became suspicious of "broke out even." I always noticed that for many days following that particular statement, I never saw meat on the table.

* * * *

Did my mother love her poker games more than she loved me? Because of what happened at our Sunday picnic at Gregson Hot Springs near Butte, I had reason to believe so.

Here's the story: A few of us kids were playing with some leftover carnival equipment while our mothers were busy with poker at a nearby table. Accidentally, I struck myself in the face with an iron tent stake I used to pound down on one of those contraptions that causes a hunk of metal to run up a pole and ring a bell. The rubber strike area bounced the iron stake back to my face, and I still have a small scar on my nose to show for it.

14

I wasn't hurt badly, but I was bleeding. I ran to my mother and pleaded, "Ma, I'm hurt and I'm bleeding." My mother looked at me, and then she looked at her cards and said, "Wait just a minute."

I couldn't believe what I heard. My mother didn't jump up in hysterics and come to my rescue. Ordinarily, she'd fuss over any injury I ever had, even a tiny scratch with a drop of oozing blood, and now I'm bleeding on my face and she doesn't budge from her poker game.

At the time, I didn't forgive my mother for that, but later I softened my attitude. As a poker player myself, I could understand her feelings. I learned that at the moment I rushed to her, she had just drawn a third ace to fill out a full house and that someone "checked" and then someone "raised" and then my mother "raised" and then someone "called."

She won the pot and this made her happy; she was still smiling while she nursed my wound.

God could not be everywhere and therefore
he made mothers.
– Jewish proverb

The butcher was the rabbi
(or)
The rabbi was the butcher

There were not enough Jews living in Butte to support a full-time orthodox rabbi, so Rabbi Zuckerman opened a kosher meat market on South Main Street, and he did his own slaughtering. He was a typical old-time kosher butcher with leather cuffs, a white smock, and a yarmulke. He was always chewing on something that was white, and it wasn't gum. Sawdust covered the floor to catch any dripping blood. And since Zuckerman was familiar with cutting and sharp knives, he was also the *mohel* who performed the *brises*. Translation: He did the ceremonial circumcisions.

My mother – one of his steady customers – always complained that Zuckerman practiced shorting. She said one of his ways of shorting was to sneak his thumb onto the scale and, according to my mother, she paid for his thumb many times over. Some of the other customers also claimed that the rabbi shorted them, and several of the young Jewish men born in Butte – referring to their *brises* – made the same claim.

Boggie's mother

My brother, Hank, had two best friends – Boggie McKee and Richy Gamble. We saw a lot of Boggie because he lived close to our house on Wyoming Street, and there was another reason we saw more of Boggie – he frequently ate dinner with us because often, when he'd come home from elementary school, his mother would be gone; and the reason for this was that she was periodically arrested for selling beer she made at home.

Poor Boggie, a nice, mild fellow. He had a loving mother who had her own way of supporting her son, and he accepted it, though it embarrassed him.

When he'd show up at our house around dinnertime, we always knew his mother had been pinched.

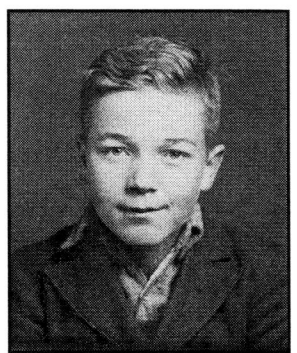

Boggie

Butte: the city, the lives, the class reunions

My entire world was this small copper-mining town nestled on the western slopes of the steep Rocky Mountains Continental Divide. As I saw it at that time, all the rest of the country was unknown territory way out there with no bearing on my life. The mines were on a hill north of the business district, and since the hill was laden with copper ore, Butte called itself "The Richest Hill on Earth." The motto is still around on some souvenir items, even though the hill was mined away, leaving behind

Main Street, looking north toward Walkerville

an enormous cavity called the Berkeley Pit.

Butte was also known as the "friendly city," and that probably was the truth, or close to it. Everyone said hello to everyone, and neighbors were always willing to help one another. Many people never locked their doors, and I can't recall having a key for any of our houses. Shopkeepers were congenial and took time to make small talk with anyone who walked in. Unlike today's national scene, serious crime was not rampant. Stealing, drunkenness, and fighting were the general infractions.

Gambling and prostitution were wide open. There was more money stacked on the gaming tables at Walker's or the Board of Trade than at the tellers' counters in the Metals Bank. The Red-Light District on Mercury and Galena streets with its cribs was clean and orderly. The going price at that time was one silver dollar or a paper dollar, although paper dollars were seldom seen.

During my school days, Butte's population was about 42,000, the largest city in the state, a metropolis compared to some of the surrounding communities, such as Whitehall, Divide, Opportunity, Basin, Dewey, Melrose, and Rocker. Most of Butte's adults were immigrants, primarily Irish, Cornish, Yugoslavian, Italian, Scandinavian, German, Greek, and French, establishing Butte as one of the nation's most diverse melting pots of European cultures.

My people, the Jewish, were a true minority, probably around 35 immigrant families at the time. I didn't know of any Jewish person who worked in the copper mines, except for my brother, Sam, for a brief time. The majority of the Jewish people were entrepreneurs of some sort, and a few were professionals in the medical field. They had clothing, furniture, and jewelry stores, a delivery service, a butcher shop, a second-hand store, and one person, who occasionally boarded at our house, was a furrier. The most interesting to us kids was a cigar maker, Mr. Hoffner, whom we watched put cigars together by using a semicircle cutter to shape the wrappers.

The Jewish residents in Butte I remember are Halpern, Goldberg, Zuckerman, Rafish, Jaffe, Ehrlich, Katz, Gordon, Ginsberg, Hoffner, Deitch, Rosenberg, Heilbronner, Riedinger, Kemper, Moran, Lippman, Susser, Finberg, Rudolph, and Gronfein.

It was easy to recognize the Yugoslavian population. Most of their names ended in "ich." There were Popovich, Milodragovich, Yovetich, Babich, O'Billovich, Bukvich, Mufich, Ducich, Tomich, and many others. Yugoslavs were the best athletes in everything – football, basketball, and track. I was a high hurdler and long jumper on the Butte High School varsity track team, but was only on the third team in football and basketball, so I jokingly told my friends that I'd have a better chance to make those varsities if I changed my name to Lowneyovich. (For additional reference on Butte's racial make-up, see piece on page 120.)

Living in Butte, and particularly growing up in Butte, is special, we were always told. It's something that gets in your blood. One of the sayings around Butte was: "If you go away, you'll always come back." But another saying was: "If you don't go away, you'll end up in the copper mines."

Gradually, all of our family left Butte. We didn't want to relive the stinging winters when the temperatures sometimes dropped to 40 below, and we didn't like the lack of career opportunities. My sister, Lee, and my brother, Sam, moved to San Francisco, and Sam later came to Seattle, as did my mother and father. My other brother, Hank, and I went off to the University of Montana at Missoula. Except for my father, who died early in life in Seattle, we've all been back to Butte – but for visits only.

But remembrance of Butte is precious, especially if a childhood was as happy and carefree as mine. I rarely miss a Butte High School reunion. Here's an opportunity to feel my roots and, through my classmates, get in touch with whom I was. Class reunions have a way of binding us into a bygone social hierarchy, and we tend to obey the pecking order of what we were during those school days. Regardless of any differences in social and economic status today, in that banquet room we still pay homage to the athletic star, the class president, or just the one with personality who made us laugh.

As many others have probably observed about class reunions, some of the plainer girls in school improved as years went by, and some of the beautiful ones didn't. One theory is that the plainer ones worked harder at making themselves more attractive, both physically and mentally. Take the case of Dollye Ogle. At school we gave her the nickname "Fried Onions" because, as one of us put it: "Her face looked like a plate of fried onions." By contrast, there was another girl in our class who had a face like an angel: perfect features framed with flowing black hair and, to use a cliche – a complexion like pink rose petals in a bowl of cream. For many of us, dating her was a wish without fulfillment.

At our thirtieth class reunion, guess who was the shining light and guess who wasn't? Dollye Ogle had a trim figure, a youthful face, and an outgoing, winning personality, and the beautiful one with a face like an angel was overweight and dissipated with bloated features like a veteran alcoholic, and she didn't have much to say. But in the banquet room I treated her with the awe as I did in yesteryear, and I had the feeling she expected it.

Ten years later, I looked forward to seeing Dollye again, and as it happens at many class reunions, we feel pain when people we like don't survive. I felt a sharp loss because I had always liked Dollye Ogle, even when she was called "Fried Onions."

On the subject of survival and class reunions, there is usually a list, posted on a board, of those who are gone. At each reunion I rush to the board to see if my name is on it. It's my standard bit of gallows humor when I remark to a classmate, "Am I relieved – my name isn't on the list."

Going to a class reunion allows me to move back in time and feel sentimental. I always rent a car and drive around to all the houses we lived in and try to visualize my life in a backward look through the years. It did seem we moved a lot, which I disliked. It meant getting new friends and neighbors and making new adjustments. The joke was: "We always moved when the rent was due," and the other joke goes: "I don't think my parents liked me too well. They'd move while I was in school, and they'd never leave a note on the door to say where."

Mostly, I remember our house at 315 Upton Street. There were six of us in a small frame house with one bedroom, one bathroom and a rollout bed. With so many personalities living in this small space, each with an agenda, disputes and arguments were a living condition, especially at the dinner table when we were all together.

But despite it all, it was a good time of life for me: I was into high school sports; and in successive years, I was vice-president of the sophomore and junior classes of more than 400 students; I had a lot of friends, and though I didn't work at it, girls seemed to like me, and this pleased my mother, who bragged about my many phone calls from girls.

Some winters were so cold, we didn't go outside; and sometimes school was canceled if a wind-chill factor left the buildings unheated. We were confined to our little house. In those days, television was only a theory, so we found other ways to pass the time. Often I'd put my warm fingers on the ice-covered windows and make designs by melting the ice. Sometimes we played cards, read, or listened to the radio. Once in a while we'd play war by building forts constructed from dominoes and by using tanks made from empty wooden sewing spools. To make a tank, we'd notch the edges of a spool and then run a rubber band through the center, anchor it on one end, put a matchstick through the rubber band at the other end, and then supply power for the tank by twirling the matchstick. As the rubber band unwound, the tank would move forward. I wonder – do kids make tanks like this anymore? Maybe not; but why would they, when there's Toys 'R' Us?

I spent much of my time reading such favorites as the stories of the Arabian nights, fairy tales of all sorts, *Æsop's Fables*, and any comic books I could buy or borrow, especially *Bringing Up Father, Mutt 'N' Jeff, Popeye,* and *Tillie the Toiler*.

But most of my life was centered around school and sports. At Butte High School, the guys would consider anyone a sissy if he didn't go out for sports. I tried all three – football, basketball, and track because it was expected of me and it was what my older brother, Hank, did, and I copied him. I showed up for all the practices and I tried hard, but the best I could do was the third team in football and basketball. I don't know how I survived football without injury. We practiced on a dirt field, which turned to mud after a rain, and when the mud dried, it was like concrete.

In track, I was on the varsity team running the high hurdles and doing the long jump, which in those days we called the broad jump. I probably made the team because, as our coach, Swede Dahlberg said, "This is the worst track team I've ever had." He didn't even want our picture taken for the high school annual. However, I did win a bronze medal for third place in the broad jump at a regional meet in Great Falls.

But it was in the high hurdles at the all-state meet at Missoula that I expected to earn my letter. I qualified for the finals and I was proud to see my name in type in the Butte paper, *The Montana Standard*. The day of the race I woke up with my legs so stiff I could hardly move them without pain, but I was so excited and eager that I didn't care about the pain. I ran a good race, but knocked over three hurdles, which disqualified me. Well, that was that. But at least I'd get my picture in the high school annual because whether Swede Dahlberg liked it or not, pictures of varsity teams – even lousy teams – were *pro forma* for the annual. However, my bad luck was still holding. Rarely did I ever miss a day of school, but the day I was out, was the day the picture was taken.

As I poke around Butte today at class reunions, it's sometimes hard to imagine living there. Gone is the bustle of the uptown* business district and the lively gambling halls – Walkers and The Board of Trade…the popular Italian restaurants in Meaderville…the streetcar rides to the Columbia Gardens…the famous Red Light District…and the hustle and spirit of a booming mining town.

Today, uptown appears rather bleak and weary, but it still holds the municipal buildings: the jail, the courthouse, and

---

*Butte people refer to the business district as "uptown" rather than the dictionary definition "downtown," probably because in Butte this area is located on the upper part of a hill.

the library. The core of Butte living has moved to the "flat" where buildings and homes are more modern and there is activity from tourism and conventions.

Those children now living in Butte are making their own memories, which will be precious to them in a backward look from their futures; but to me, Butte as it is now is a foreign land compared to what it was when it encompassed my whole life: my family, my friends, my schoolmates, and my dreams.

Even though Butte has changed, I see it in my mind as the city it was. Would I have stayed in Butte? Perhaps, if I had found a promising job after graduating from the university. I'm glad I didn't. But I do like to go back once in a while and dwell in yesteryears.

From younger to older is not a quantum leap from one time to another as if there were two separate persons; rather, it is the sum of one person – millisecond after millisecond after millisecond – all threaded together in a continuum known as lifetime.

The girl – who was she?

It was a clear summer evening before sunset, and Charlie Judd and I – both seniors at Butte High School – had little to do except walk up and down Park Street searching for anything of interest. We stopped in the center of town, Park and Main, in front of the Metals Bank Building, and just looked around and chatted.

Suddenly our mouths closed and our eyes were fixed in the same direction. Here was a girl (we never called a grown, young female a woman) walking on the other side of the street. She was nobody we'd ever seen before, perhaps about 18 or 19, possibly a visitor. Something about her presence totally consumed our male awareness in a sort of tandem consciousness in which two minds held the same thoughts.

Something like this

Her light tawny hair touching her shoulders glistened from rays of sun nearing the horizon. She was trim and wore a simple pink dress that clung, but not too tightly, to her shape. But it was her walk that spoke out, because there was a graceful and regal manner about it that seemed to say, "I know who I am and I like myself and I am a good-natured person." Could a walk say that much? It did to me. Her head was up, and her posture was correct, and with a wisp of a smile, she moved effortlessly along the sidewalk as if the walk were put there especially for her footsteps. Her hair, crowning her more-than-pretty face, bounced slightly in cadence with her steps.

After the traffic light changed, she crossed to the corner where we were standing. For me – and I think for Charlie, too – her presence made the street seem more pleasant, just as would a sudden breeze with the scent of lilacs. She smiled at us with the sort of smile that was simply a "hello" and not an invitation. Charlie and I didn't speak. We were totally absorbed by this vision standing nearby as though we were drawn into her aura.

It must have been too much for Charlie. He walked over to her and let words come out he could-n't contain any longer. He said, "Are you God?"

She looked at Charlie with a friendly smile but didn't speak. The light changed to green and she was gone.

*Charlie
and Paul*

The Coca-Cola culture

Coca-Cola was the focal point of our after-school-hours socializing near Butte High. It was our mantra. Not the Coke in bottles or cans, but the kind mixed at a soda fountain from Coke syrup and carbonated water. It was five cents a glass. Adding another flavor to the Coke was the "in thing." Only a square who didn't understand our tribal mores would order a plain Coke. It was usually a cherry

Coke or chocolate Coke, sometimes lemon or lime. Cherry was the favorite.

The scene was Paxson and Rockefeller Drug Store on West Park Street, where we chatty juveniles crowded the counter and tables and sipped our Cokes amid a cacophony of conversations, laughter, music, clinking glasses, and the constant hiss of soda water squirting into glasses. Girls usually dressed in skirts and sweaters and the boys in slacks and sweaters or jackets. By today's standards, our appearance – and our speech – would seem old-fashioned and corny because our dress and grooming was neat and clean and devoid of straggly hair and sloppiness and grunge, and our speech was lacking in gutter talk and not punctuated with the vocal hesitations of "you know" and the repetitive stereotypes of "cool," "man," "like," "I mean," and "awesome." Of course, we had a few stereotypes of our own, such as "neat," "nuts," "keen," "hot dog," "scram," and "whoopee," but we didn't use them as addictive verbal crutches.

But one element remains standard and suffers no change in the passage of years – it's the fondness for Coca-Cola and the social centerpiece it provides while giving a small lift. This affair with Coke appears to be eternal, even though, at present, some turncoats have deserted Coca-Cola for an upstart named Pepsi.

Does Yiddish say it better?

If Butte children of foreign-born parents from mainland Europe were like the kids in our family, they understood, at least basically, the language of their parents, whether it be Yugoslavian, Italian, Greek, Finnish, etc. Yiddish mixed with English is what we heard at home, and lately, I've noticed something special about Yiddish: When I want to use a negative or disparaging term to describe a person, I sometimes find myself thinking in Yiddish.

I wondered about this. Is it because Yiddish – compared to English – appears to have a larger inventory of such words, and if so, is it because, in a long history of oppression, Jews developed words to vent their feelings and to taunt their oppressors? Or is it that during my youthful, impressionable years in Butte, the use of Yiddish words around our home had a strong impact on my mind? Or is it that there is a depth of feelings in the Jewish makeup that brings out certain nuances in Yiddish "negative" words that defines more closely the foibles and anomalies in the human character?

For instance, the Yiddish word *nudnick* has a more vivid meaning to me than the word "pest"; and the same for *goilem* for a "stupid" person, and *shnorrer* for a "moocher."

The idea of putting together a list of these words intrigued me. I searched my childhood memories of Butte and visualized my parents speaking Yiddish as if I was watching an old movie. The words I remembered gave me a substantial number for my list, but I knew that there were many I didn't recall, so help came from some of my Jewish friends in Seattle who grew up in homes with Yiddish-speaking (Ashkenazi) parents.

The English spelling of all the words written in a different alphabet (transliteration) posed a problem. Fortunately, someone gave me a helpful resource for this – Leo Rosten's scholarly and highly readable book, *The Joys of Yiddish*. Not only did the book provide some needed spellings, but it yielded additional words that were missing from my list. Also helpful were Seattle residents, Rabbi William Greenberg and a teacher of Yiddish, Ruth Peizer.

Mr. Rosten aptly makes the point that many Yiddish words have entered – and enriched – our English language, and I might add, especially in and around New York City. Here are some Americanized words that appear in my *Webster's Ninth New Collegiate Dictionary*: *gonif, schlock, schlepp, chutzpa, schlemiel.*

The vulgar words, which I didn't hear around our home, but among Jewish males, are listed separately at the end.

MY LIST

alter kocker	A crotchety old man.
amho'oretz	An ignoramus, a boor.
batlan	A man of no promise, a dreamer , an idler.

behayma	Literally, an animal; a stupid person, a dummy.
bulvan	A coarse, rude person.
chochem	Slang: a wise guy, a smart aleck; literally, a wise man.
chazzer	A pig, a greedy person.
draykop	One who mixes your head with talk.
dumkop	A dunce, a dumbbell.
eizel	Literally, a donkey; a fool, a dope.
farbissener	A dour one, an unpleasant one.
farblonjet	One who is lost. Bewildered.
farchadat	A dizzy, dopey person.
faygeleh	A bird; when referring to a man, a sissy-type, a homosexual.
ferd	Literally, a horse; an overstuffed person, a stolid one.
fonfer	A double-talker, talks through the nose.
fresser	An overeater.
goilem	A simpleton, a dull person.
gonif	A thief.
gozlin	A swindler, a cheat.
grober	A coarse, insensitive or fat person.
klutz	A clod, a clumsy bungler.
k'nocker	A cocky showoff.
kurveh	A bad woman, a prostitute.
kvetcher	A complainer.
mieskeit	An ugly person.

meshuggener	A crazy man.
momzer	A bastard, a detestable person.
moishe kapoyr	A contrary person who puts things backwards.
nafka	A prostitute, a street walker.
nar	A fool.
nebbish	A helpless sad sack, a pitiful person.
no-goodnik	Yiddish/English for a no-gooder.
nochshlepper	One who drags along after another, unwanted follower.
nudge	A pesky person.
nudnik	A pest, a bore, a nuisance.
ongeblozzener	A puffed-up stuffed shirt.
oysvurf	A scoundrel, a bum, an outcast.
parech	A nasty person, a low person.
proster mentsh	A vulgar, common man.
prostak	A churl, an ignorant boor.
shikker	A drunkard.
shlemiel	A loser, a foolish person, clumsy bungler.
shlepper	A drag, a freeloader.
shlimazel	Perpetually unlucky, incompetent.
shmendrik	A pipsqueak of no account, a dope.
shlumper	An untidy, messy person.
shnook	A gullible, sappy person.
shmegegi	A fool, a drip of no consequence.
shmo	A boob, a naïve person.
shnorrer	A moocher

shtunk	A nasty person, a stinker.
szhlop	A moron.
tsedrayter	A mixed-up, confused person.
yachna	A gossiping woman.
yekl	A sucker, a stupid person.
yold	A boob, a simpleton.
zhlub	A coarse, clumsy person.

VULGAR LIST

pisher	A young squirt of no consequence, literally, a urinator.
putz	A penis; a jerk.
shmuck	A penis, a putz, a detestable man.
shtik drek	A s_ _ _ head.
yentzer	A promiscuous copulator.

Though we children didn't speak the Yiddish we heard at home, we did understand it, and so did our dog, Freddy.

My friends – the ants

$\mathbf{A}$s a preschool child – living on Iowa Street, the first residence I can remember – I was always friendly towards ants. They were my companions. I'd watch them constantly as they went in and out of their hole alongside my neighbor's fence, depositing grains of sand on a mound. They were small black ants, and I was careful not to step on one. If accidentally I did step on an ant, the smashed body on the sidewalk looked like a drop of rain, and as I recall, there was a saying that if you stepped on an ant, it would rain.

When the air grew chilly and winter approached, I was concerned about the ants down in that hole. Winters in Butte are bitingly frigid, sometimes reaching 40 degrees below zero. Wouldn't the poor ants freeze to death in the frozen ground? I didn't want that to happen because I looked forward to seeing them again in the spring.

In my child's mind, I thought I could help keep them warm by insulating the top of their hole. I covered it with pieces of rag and hunks of burlap and anchored the cloth with sticks I drove into the ground. Surely this would keep out the cold.

Our neighbor was a kindly man, but he was not pleased with this eyesore of cloth and sticks against his fence. I explained to him that I was doing an act of kindness to keep the ants warm during the bitter oncoming winter.

36

He didn't ridicule me, but he explained to me very factually that the ants have their own way of surviving in the ground and that the cloth covering wouldn't make any difference and that my ants would be back next spring. Then he asked me to remove the construction I had made.

I was not sure he was telling me the truth, so he told me to ask my parents about it. My father was a scientific type of man who read a lot, and he assured me that our neighbor was right.

It was only after this assurance that I removed the covering and threw it in the garbage can. My neighbor was pleased, and he was right. The ants came out of their hole in the spring, and I was glad to see them.

There is a miracle in life – even in the tiniest
creature – even in a bacterium

Elizabeth Leonard
a love story

*E*lizabeth "Liz" Leonard came into my life through my older brother, Hank, who dated her older sister, Jane. At the time, I was home in Butte on summer break from my junior year at the University of Montana in Missoula. Some of my most poignant and lasting memories of Montana are of Elizabeth, with whom there was strong mutual affection, bathing my mind with warm thoughts, which to this day, still linger. Despite all her beauty and talent in dancing, music and oil painting, Liz was modest and reserved, and to me, looked more beautiful than ever when seated at her piano, filling the room with the stirring tones of Rachmaninoff's *Prelude in C-sharp Minor*. We often felt that our affection for each other was so strong and intuitive that sometimes we knew each other's unspoken thoughts. Ours was a pristine, youthful love, uncalloused by the realities of experience.

There was a tender vulnerability about Elizabeth and a touch of sadness as if she was weeping over all the pain that visits Earth's creatures, including herself. She was a caring soul who lived with both the sweetness and the bitterness of life, and who seemed to view existence with an innocent wonderment of, "What do I want from life and what does life want from me?"

Liz and I would sit on counter stools at the Grand Silver store soda fountain on Park Street, talking endlessly about school, our hopes and ambitions, and our growing affection for each other. Whenever I could borrow the family car, a Dodge sedan, I'd park in a desolate area west of the School of Mines and we'd hold each other close without letup, as though each treasured moment we were not touching was a wasted moment. At a time and place in which abstinence was the prevailing norm, Elizabeth and I were among the innocents. Sometimes, after a long emotional embrace, she would sigh, "Oh, Tidy," as if these words were a release for feelings suddenly bursting free, and a salve for those still in bondage. Tidy was Liz's long-time nursemaid with whom Liz developed an affectionate and supportive need. My oneness with Elizabeth was so complete, I felt that her life was also my life, and the simple expression "Oh, Tidy" became part of my being, too, and for many years, whenever I felt overwhelmed with emotion – either joy, fear, or frustration – I would sometimes utter, "Oh, Tidy."

In retrospect, my all-too-brief time with Elizabeth was a pure joy – a joy which taught me that the pain in life can find compensation by the joy in life; and more: because of the untried, naïve nature of my youth, my joy was unfettered by any sense of responsibility or doubt, and was fresh and new, arising from feelings which have only one first time in any one lifetime.

After graduating from the University of Montana, I moved to San Francisco where I found a job as a trainee for the Dean Witter securities firm. Somehow, through distance and circumstances, Liz and I lost each other, but what was not lost, however, was the image of her living in my mind so vividly, I would sometimes see her face among the passers-by crowding the sidewalks of San Francisco. After work, I would ride the Market Street streetcar from the financial center to the Mission District, where I had a small, antiquated room, and sometimes during the ride, I would scribble in a small notebook. One time – amid the cacophony of the traffic din and the streetcar's incessant clanging bell – I wrote this little poem for Liz:

Of life and time:
Life is when I'm with you.
Time is all the spaces in between.

During this time, I read Robert Nathan's *Portrait of Jennie*, a beautifully told love story with supernatural overtones, and I imagined Liz was Jennie and I was Eben, although, unlike the book, our ages were close, since I was only two years older. For me, the following passage in the book, in a somewhat mystical manner, resonated the feelings between Liz and me: *What is it which makes a man and a woman know that they, of all other men and women in the world, belong to each other? Is it no more than chance and meeting? no more than being alive together in the world at the same time? . . . Or is it something deeper and stranger, something beyond meeting, something beyond chance and fortune? Is there, perhaps, one soul among all others – among all who have lived in endless generations, who must love us, and whom we must love . . . whom we must seek all our lives long . . . ?*

Did I ever try to find Elizabeth? Not as hard as I should have. In my mind, Liz was in a far-off world, and with my meager pay, I was struggling to make a career for myself, and at that time, I never entertained any serious thoughts beyond a single life. Through the years, I would ask Butte people if they knew the whereabouts of Elizabeth or the Leonard family, the family who lived on West Galena Street and operated a florist shop. No one knew. Apparently, I asked the wrong people, and I accepted the reality that I would never find Elizabeth.

Now, let's move from the past to the year 2000. I made a brief mention of Elizabeth in the previous printing of this book, in a section titled, "The unforgettables." I did this because my memories of her were precious and a significant part in my emerging maturity in Butte; but there was another reason: I was hoping the printed words somehow would lead to information about where she was and how she was; and hope against hope, that I could find her and fill the emptiness that comes when a cherished person vanishes; and also, I was hoping that finding her would allow me to put into place the person of my memories with the person of today.

The few sentences in the book were successful. Last summer, shortly after the second printing of this volume, my phone in Seattle rang, and a woman said with emotion and feeling: "This is Barbara Johnson in Grapevine, Texas. I am Elizabeth Leonard's daughter. A friend of mine in Butte, Gene Costello, sent me your Butte book and I was moved to tears over the kind and wonderful words you wrote about my mother. It meant so much to me." I then sensed what was coming and I hoped my senses were wrong. "Mother died seven years ago. She often spoke of you." This news was not totally unexpected. How could I react to it? Not so much with words as with feelings. One void in my life was filled, and another void was created.

Barbara (Mrs. James Johnson) recited a summary of Liz's life: two marriages, three children, lived in San Diego where she earned critical praise for her Western-theme portraits and landscapes, and where she is buried following a struggle with cancer. Barbara sent me photocopies of pictures of Elizabeth taken during the passing of years.

The occasional phone calls and mail from a delightful Barbara are my slim thread to the life of Elizabeth. At present, we have a *quid pro quo* arrangement: I send her copies of my books, and from Grapevine, Texas, she sends me one of my favorite foods – Texas chili.

Every lifetime is littered with "what if,"
"should have done," and "might have been."

Incident at Ott's Grocery

My parents were Jewish immigrants from Lithuania who came through Ellis Island many years ago. My father was from Kretinga on the Baltic, and my mother was from a small village near Kovno. They met in Glasgow, Scotland, where they married, came to America traveling steerage, and eventually moved to Butte.

Unlike today, when a foreign accent is considered cosmopolitan and diversity is fashionable, in those days, immigrants from non-English-speaking countries in Europe were called "greenhorns" and were tolerated as intruders.

I must admit that as a self-centered little kid, I was a bit ashamed of my parents' Jewish accent when they came into contact with my schoolmates from American parents. One incident concerning my mother's speech caused me an embarrassment that stays in my mind with vivid remembrance.

She sent me to Ott's Grocery for what she said was a box of "oytmeal" so I said to Mr. Ott (who was a bit of an anti-Semite as I now view it), "I'd like a large box of oytmeal." He said, "What's that?" I said, "My mother said to get oytmeal." He said, "What?" and again I said "oytmeal." Finally, he said, "Oh, you mean oatmeal," and then he started to laugh. My face turned red. He kept chuckling, and then his partners in the store began laughing too. I was doubly mad: Mad at them for making fun of me and mad at my mother for sending me into this embarrassment.

When I came home with the oatmeal, I said to my mother, "They teased me at the store because I asked for oytmeal, and it's not oytmeal, it's oatmeal. They made me feel like a little greenhorn, and it's all your fault. I wish you'd learn to speak English."

My mother, who spoke broken English with a Yiddish accent but couldn't read or write English, seemed hurt and said, "I'm sorry my English is not so good and I don't get all my words right, but I wasn't born in this country. I'm not as lucky as you are." I looked at my mother for a moment and my annoyance subsided and I said, "It's all right, Ma. It doesn't matter. They made me feel bad in that store. I'll never go in there again." And I never did.

Carol's surprise

Carol

Carol Heilbronner, one of the girls from the upper-income Westside, always approached me with more than friendship, but friendship was all I responded to, because at the time, I was totally consumed with the beauty and charms of another student, Marjorie Fennimore (see page 106), but was always too shy to do anything about it.

Carol's father owned a printing company and he was rich enough to buy her a car. Time and again Carol offered me a ride home from Butte High School, although the walk wasn't that far. Every time she gave me a ride, I would never let her take me all the way home. I'd always say, "I want to visit Creighton." He was my classmate who lived in a big house in a middle-class neighborhood on South Main Street. She would let me out at Creighton's house, and if he wasn't in, I'd simply walk home after Carol was out of sight.

One time Carol said, "Every time I try to give you a ride

46

home, I never take you all the way; you always get off at Creighton's. This time, I want to take you home and I want to meet your parents."

I was caught with no way out. I didn't want her to meet my immigrant parents with their Yiddish accents, and I didn't want her to see our small house in a low-rent neighborhood. I was a little snob who was popular with the rich kids and I didn't want to spoil it.

But I was stuck. Carol came into our house on Upton Street, and I introduced her to my mother, who was the only one home at the time. My mother was totally gracious toward Carol and was happy that such a nice-looking, well-groomed girl with a car was friendly toward her youngest son.

Well, it's done now, I thought to myself. She saw our home, she met my immigrant mother and now she knows I'm Jewish, and that's that. I don't care. She's only a friend, and besides, I am emotionally drawn to Marjorie Fennimore.

I walked Carol to her car and before she drove away she said, "Your mother is a wonderful, warm person, and you should be glad you have such a good mother who is so proud of you. Now here's something you don't know. I'm Jewish, too. My parents were born in this country, but their parents were immigrants from Germany." What a surprise! Carol was Jewish, too. From then on, I felt close to Carol, and she became my special friend forever.

A lesson at the blackboard

If you are like me, one of the pains in life is not being believed when you are telling the total and absolute truth. Add to this mental injury a touch of physical pain and, voilá!, you have planted an emotional seed that blossoms into a memory lasting a lifetime. Is it because deeper feelings make stronger impressions in the brain? Probably. Even though this event was trivial, it eventually became important simply because, in recall, it survived a kaleidoscope of happenings in my life that, as years flew by, fell into a black hole of oblivion, leaving no trace in the mind.

This is the scene as if it occurred just yesterday. During a grammar lesson at Monroe Elementary School, I wrote a few sentences on the blackboard. Miss Riley, our fourth-grade, no-nonsense teacher – a short and stocky one we called "The Little Corporal" – told me to put dots above my "j"s. Well, I knew about a dot above an "i", but truly was unaware of a dot for a "j", and I said, "I didn't know a 'j' had a dot." Miss Riley, apparently thinking I was trying to be cute, stabbed my temple a couple of times with a long piece of chalk and said, "Don't be a wise guy in my classroom." It hurt. How unfair. She didn't believe me. I swallowed my anger, and it was soon gone, but not the memory. I'll always remember standing at the blackboard and "The Little Corporal" and that, definitely, a "j" has a dot.

My father, a free thinker

I write more about my mother in Butte than about my father because my father died early in his life and my time around him was short, and besides, my mother was the dominating influence in our household. My father remained aloof, being content to work hard at his small plumbing business for meager amounts of money, which he turned over – every cent – to my mother.

I do remember that my father was a scientific type of man who was a total free thinker. He always said the world was flat, and I guess from a commonsense viewpoint, that opinion is logical. After all, looking out in the distance,

nobody can see a curve. My father was wrong about the Earth being flat, but he would have been right if he had said the universe was flat because now, the strong belief among cosmologists is that the universe – thought to be curved – continues to inflate at such a rapid rate, that this enormous inflation smoothes out the curves.

Also, my father didn't believe in gravity. He said that if objects fall to earth, like an apple from a tree, it isn't because of gravity; it's because the objects are heavier than air. He said a gas balloon is lighter than air and therefore doesn't fall to earth. A very logical man.

I only wish my father had lived long enough to see the photos of our planet taken by the astronauts. Certainly he would see the world is round. And as for gravity, he would see objects heavier than air floating around the shuttle cabin where gravity is not a factor.

My father treated me like there was something special about me, perhaps because I was the youngest, and also because I would sympathize with his scientific theories.

From the bits of conversation I gleaned, my father was born in Kretinga, Lithuania, had little or no schooling, and left home at the age of 15 and found work on an English merchant ship. He taught himself to read and write English and was an avid reader, especially science, politics, and true detective stories.

In Butte, I can't recall that my father ever went to a movie. He didn't care for movie actors because he said he could never figure out why they were paid more than the president, when in his opinion, all actors ever do – and I quote directly – "is twist their faces a little." As I said before, my father was a free thinker.

He had unique ways of expressing his dislikes for a person who dressed or groomed outrageously. He would refer to them as an "article." That was his way of giving them no status. In today's climate of grunge, tattooing, metal piercing, and eyesore clothing and hairstyles, my father would be inundated with "articles."

I remember how unselfish he was – how everything he had and everything he could do were for his wife and children, not caring about what remained for himself. Mostly, what he left with me was a way of looking at life: Be an independent thinker. Don't go along with something just because everyone else does, especially if in your deepest convictions, you believe you are right, but don't disagree just for the sake of disagreeing. He told me: "If everyone in the room says 'red' and you think they're wrong, have the courage to say 'white.' " These concepts from my father are still a part of me, and the influence of his beliefs, his wonderment, and his questions about the world were the driving force for me to pursue my academic studies in philosophy and my private studies in science. As to where all this brought me: My philosophies are part idealism, part pragmatism, and part skepticism, and I hope they always include objectivity and reasonableness.

I'm sure that my father, and also my mother, felt that their struggling lives as uneducated immigrants were not that significant when measured by achievement. If my parents were here today, they would be proud of the accomplishments of their children and grandchildren: two physicists, one neurosurgeon, three lawyers, one electrical engineer, a writer-publisher, a medical-center executive, a symphony musician, and a program director for Microsoft.

When thoughts of my father surface, my mind flashes back to a philosophy class at the University of Montana taught by Professor Marvin. I was giving an oral report on the intuitionist philosophy of Henri Bergson. There was a knock on the classroom door and I knew instinctively – almost telepathically – what that knock was all about. It would be a Western Union messenger. I sensed that my father failed to survive a serious operation earlier in the day in Seattle's Providence Hospital. I was right. I hurried to the law school building on campus and waited for my brother, Hank, to come out. My face registered my sadness, and when I said, "We're leaving for Seattle," he immediately knew what my words meant.

How vividly I remember my father's burial in Seattle. Since none of us children had any religious upbringing, it was my first encounter with an orthodox Jewish burial. I had never heard the Kaddish, a Hebrew mourning prayer, which began: *Yis'ga'dal v'yis'kadash sh'may ra'bbo, b'olmo dee'vro chir'usay v'yamlich malchu'say, b'chayaychon uv'y-omay'chon uv'chayay d'chol bais Yisroel, ba'agolo u'viz'man koriv; v'imru Omein....* I had no yarmulke and neither did my brother, Hank, so someone loaned us felt hats. Mine was too large, and so was Hank's. My other brother, Sam, owned a felt hat and had a good fit. I mourned my wonderful father for years to come, but at that funeral I nearly laughed out loud. As I repeated Kaddish intoned by the rabbi, my hat slipped down and rested on my ears. Hank's hat fell over his eyes, and when I looked at him, I had to suppress a giggle. In my grief, how could I find this so enormously funny? I did. I'm sorry, Pa.

After the funeral, my mother stayed on in Seattle, and now both my mother and father are buried side by side in this city. I visit the cemetery once in a while and have a quiet moment reflecting on my early life in Butte with my parents. It's the Jewish tradition to use a stone instead of flowers, so before I leave, I put a stone on each grave and walk away with a feeling of peace and a little less guilt – guilt, because I was not as good a son to my parents as I should have been.

Fortunate is the one who has a good father.

Morning mood

There must be something wrong with people who are cheerful and talkative after waking up in the morning. These people are not normal. In the morning you're supposed to be sleepy, grouchy, and non-talkative.

I had a hard time getting my mother to understand this. She'd awaken me for elementary school and ask me what I wanted for breakfast. It was the morning mantra: "Do you want pancakes, French toast, or scrambled eggs and toast?" I wouldn't answer. She'd ask again. No answer. And she would ask again and again. Finally, with the irritation of a half-asleep person who resents being awakened, I'd grumble: "Ma, you know I don't talk in the morning. Make whatever you want."

My mother was the most caring, loving mother any kid could ever have, but she had no respect for the sanctity of morning grouchiness.

The culture – then and now

Rather than guessing at specific calendar years for the pieces in this book, allow me to frame the time period by defining aspects of culture during this bygone era.

To be specific: Many of the automobiles had to be hand-cranked (being careful to retard the spark lest you break an arm) and cars had running-boards, and most of the brand names have long since disappeared: *Franklin, Packard, Hupmobile, La Salle, Nash, Pierce Arrow, Reo, Studebaker, Cord, Hudson, Whippet, Essex, Model-T Ford*, and a few others. The price of a mid-size car was around $1,000 or less. Hamburgers were 15¢, hot dogs a dime, a loaf of bread 12¢, and gas around 19¢ or 20¢ a gallon. A full-course Sunday dinner at the new, fancy Finlen Hotel was a dollar,

Main Street, looking south.

which also happened to be the price of a woman in the cribs in the Red Light District on Mercury and Galena streets.

An example of some of the technology at that time: Dial telephones were on the verge of coming in, but not in time for my early childhood. The first phone I used was attached to the wall, and when I took the receiver off the hook, a female voice cooed, "Number please," and after I gave her the number she always repeated it back with overly distinct enunciation, especially the number "nine," which always came out "nigh-own." Wagons loaded with ice blocks for the homes moved throughout the city on regular routes. There were some primitive electric refrigerators around, but we had a wooden icebox that used blocks of ice, brought in by a man with a leather wrap on his back to protect him against the cold of the melting ice which was slung over his shoulder and held with metal tongs.

It helps to explain Butte's culture by the nature of the schools. At that time, schools were a place of discipline and learning, with intensive studies in English, history, science, civics, math, personal health – and plenty of homework. There was no wising-off in class, no talking back to teachers, and no talking out loud unless called upon; however, we did manage to throw a few spitballs and pass notes around. Students were well groomed and neatly dressed; boys mostly in corduroys or overalls. Girls wore blouses or sweaters and skirts, saddle shoes, bobby sox, and girdles. For a mature girl not to wear a girdle was considered indecent.

One girl in high school I socialized with told me jokingly, "When I'm with you, Paul, I wear two girdles – one to keep me in and the other to keep you out." Of course, this was simply humor, because at the time, I was shy around girls, and my main conversation was about plans for going to college and sports: football, basketball, or track, depending on the season.

All in all, those times for me were good, and as a society, there were pluses and minuses in contrast with today's society. There was some crime, but it wasn't pandemic like today, and episodic violent crimes by children were unthinkable. Primary schools did a better job in education than today, and people were more civil to one another and less openly profane.

Families were strong, and, for better or for worse, unwed pregnancy, unwed cohabitation, and divorce were stigmas to be avoided. Television, frequently blamed for contributing to much of today's social problems, was at that time an invention awaiting an inventor. The movies we saw were mostly good cowboys versus bad cowboys and settlers versus Indians. Violence was depicted as part of the story, and unlike today, usually was not gratuitous and thrown in simply for shock value. If there had been a rating system then, all movies would carry a "G."

We did have our share of alcoholics, but of all the Butte residents I knew, none were addicted to illegal drugs, yet, at present in Seattle, I know a half dozen people – mostly young women – desperately trying to end their dependence on either heroin, cocaine, crack, crank or ice. To my knowledge, there wasn't a single case of youth suicide, a sharp contrast to the present escalated rate of such tragedies.

One minus for those times was the lack of government sensitivity and financial assistance for the poor, the mentally ill, and the physically handicapped; and another minus came from a certain amount of overt and covert discrimination against non-whites, females, and those of certain religions.

As for today, be thankful that we enjoy a more caring public sector, less discrimination, and giant advances in medicine, nutrition, and health care; and people are living longer – that is, if they don't get murdered.

If we move ten steps forward and nine steps backward, there is progress.

A guru for all seasons – Louis Forsell

An eager mind is like a seed, yearning to grow; a good teacher is like a gardener who nourishes the seed until it blossoms.

Louis

Everyone should have a Louis Forsell in his life – someone who opens windows in the mind, broadens horizons of knowledge, and teaches the satisfaction and joy in appreciating classical music, prose, and poetry.

I met Louis during my junior year in high school through a girl I dated on a friendship basis, Hannajane Israel. Hannajane's older brother, Billy, was a friend of Louis, and Louis always seemed to be around the Israel household when I called for Hannajane. They were usually drinking tea and discussing intellectual-type subjects that were strange to my ears, and soon I was joining their discussions over cups of tea.

I had little knowledge of the arts, only bits and pieces I learned at school and from my sister, who talked about *I Pagliacci* and opera, so listening to Louis and Billy was like a humanities seminar in dialogue form. I was fascinated with their discussions of prose by Thomas Wolfe, Ernest Hemingway, Lincoln Steffens, and poetry by Ernest Dowson, John Masefield, Robert Browning, and music by Sibelius, Tchaikovsky, Bartok, and Beethoven.

How could these two, only a year ahead of me in school, know all this? Why didn't I have this knowledge? We all lived in Butte and went to Butte High School. Soon I forgot about Hannajane and came to the Israel house for teacup discussions – and speaking of the tea, there was a little game they played – how many cups can be strained from one tea bag? Usually it came to three and a half.

Louis's god was Hemingway. It was "Hemingway this and Hemingway that." I was not a fan of some of Hemingway's beliefs, especially his approval of bull fighting. But I did take the time to memorize the words of John Donne in the preface to *For Whom the Bell Tolls*, and I still recite it now and then.

I was more fascinated with Thomas Wolfe, whose prose was brilliant and lyrical, almost like music to my ears. Often I have thought of his words as an artist's brush bringing to life images like beautiful paintings. My favorite was his *Look Homeward, Angel*. In this book I enjoyed the river of sentences as they flowed on effortlessly, sometimes without my thinking about the meaning of the words.

With Louis's guidance, I found a musical treasure in Sibelius's *Finlandia* and *Valse Triste* and Tchaikovsky's *Sixth* and Beethoven's *Fifth* and *Ninth*; and to this day I have never abandoned this music or grown tired of it.

But it was Louis's poetry that became a part of me – the poetry he had written when he was lovesick and failing with a classmate, Jeannie; and the poetry he memorized from other authors and recited constantly. At that time, I found it exceptionally easy to hear something and hold it in my memory. My favorite is one by Ernest Dowson, *Non Sum Qualis Eram Bonae sub Regno Cynarae.*

Of his original poetry, I still remember one he wrote to Jeannie after she rejected him. It goes:

> *Saucy Jeannie,*
> *You dodge my snares*
> *Illusively as a nuthatch*
> *Flitting through the trees,*
> *But I'll weave a web of fine silk words*
> *And trap you as I please,*
> *And then as the water ouzel*
> *Pounces upon his prey*
> *Shall I descend upon you*
> *And gloat at your dismay*
> *While my love eats you away.*

Another one to Jeannie went something like this:

> *Lost: one heart.*
> *I suspect, you, Jeannie, of having found it.*
> *It has several lacerations,*
> *So handle it with care.*
> *It is delicate and perishable,*
> *So please put it in the refrigerator*
> *Where it will keep,*
> *And you better wrap it in wax paper,*
> *So it won't absorb the odors of fish, onions, and cheese,*
> *And maybe you better label it*
> *So your mother won't use it for hash.*

Through the years I thought about Louis, and as time went by, my urge to find him became stronger and stronger. I wanted to thank him for the treasures he brought me, but I lost complete contact with him. I heard that before he retired and moved away, he had married, raised three daughters, and pursued a distinguished legal career with the Montana Attorney General's Office.

There was a Forsell listed in the Butte directory. My phone call was answered by Dorothy Forsell, the widow of Louis's cousin, and from her I learned that Louis was living somewhere in Mexico; and then she gave me the address of Louis's sister, Marvel, in Hawaii. My letter to Marvel came back undelivered. Finally, Dorothy called me with Louis's phone number and address in Ajijic, a retirement community near Guadalajara, mostly Americans and Canadians.

I immediately put through a call to Mexico. I knew what I'd do. I wouldn't identify myself. I'd merely start quoting the Jeannie poem. And this is what I did when he answered the phone. He didn't react immediately, and then came the dawn. He remembered the poem and then I told him who I was, and he was totally astounded that after all these years, I carried this verse in my mind and he was thrilled to hear from me. I wanted to recite *Cynarae* to him, but I decided to save that for later. I was determined to go to Mexico and visit him, but fleeting life does not always await our plans, and a heavy shadow of remorse engulfed my being after Dorothy called with news of Louis's passing.

Let's hope that the words in this piece about Louis will reveal some of the light he gave us, and will serve as a reminder that Louis was here.

The story of Louis Forsell would not be complete without repeating Dowson's *Cynarae*, which Louis would recite over and over until, without seeing it in print, the poem became stamped on my brain, every syllable of it, and even to this day it remains a permanent part of my literary inventory; and on occasion I quote it aloud so I won't forget it. The grieving love in *Cynarae* parallels Louis's anguish over losing Jeannie and tells a true story of Dowson, who in despair over rejection by a very young Polish girl named Adelaide, searches for comfort in the arms of others.

Non Sum Qualis Eram Bonae sub Regno Cynarae
(I'm not as I was under the reign of the kind Cynarae)

Last night, ah, yesternight, betwixt her lips and mine
There fell thy shadow, Cynara! thy breath was shed
Upon my soul between the kisses and the wine;
And I was desolate and sick of an old passion,
Yea, I was desolate and bowed my head:
I have been faithful to thee, Cynara! in my fashion.
All night upon mine heart I felt her warm heart beat,
Night-long within mine arms in love and sleep she lay;
Surely the kisses of her bought red mouth were sweet;
But I was desolate and sick of an old passion,
When I awoke and found the dawn was gray:
I have been faithful to thee, Cynara! in my fashion.
I have forgot much, Cynara! Gone with the wind,

Flung roses, roses riotously with the throng,
Dancing, to put thy pale, lost lilies out of mind;
But I was desolate and sick of an old passion,
Yea, all the time, because the dance was long;
I have been faithful to thee, Cynara!! in my fashion.
I cried for madder music and for stronger wine,
But when the feast is finished and the lamps expire,
Then falls thy shadow, Cynara! the night is thine;
And I am desolate and sick of an old passion,
Yea, hungry for the lips of my desire:
I have been faithful to thee, Cynara! in my fashion.

Of our conflicts with others we make rhetoric; of
our conflicts with ourselves we make poetry.

– William Butler Yeats

The meaning of tears

When I was little, I had few social outings with my parents. Mostly, I hung around with my older brother, Hank, and my playmates, Benny Crowley and Bobby Doull. I had never heard the term "babysitter." If my older siblings didn't look after me, my mother hauled me along with her, especially to her ladies' poker parties. She'd dump me on top of the coats in the bedroom and I'd fall asleep, but not so soundly that I couldn't faintly hear the clatter of poker chips and the repetitions of "I'm in..." "check..." "raise..." "call..." "you're bluffing..." "your deal," and then later when it was feasting time, the cacophony of clanking dishes and mixed conversations, half English, half Yiddish.

Once in a while, when I was about six or seven, my mother would take me to a movie. She liked love stories, which all of us kids called "mush." We wanted action movies with cowboys and Indians and fighting. The good guy always got the girl, but he first had to win a fight. I always thought that to kiss a girl, you had to win a fight, and that in the "mush" movies, the good guys were all sissies because they could kiss the girl without fighting.

I can recall one sentimental love movie in which my mother cried a lot. She cried when it was sad, but she also cried in parts that weren't sad, such as a reconciliation of two lovers after a misunderstanding. I remember saying to my mother, "Ma (we always said "ma" instead of mother) why are you crying? This part isn't sad; it's a happy part," and she said – coming from behind her little tear-soaked handkerchief, – "I'm crying because I'm glad it didn't come out sad, and besides, I enjoy the movie more if I cry."

I thought about what she said – you can cry over sad and you can cry over happy. Everybody knows that. But why? Is it that tears – arising from a well of fervent emotions – give more substance to our deeper feelings?

A dog started my career

Freddy

Memories of my early life in Butte would not be complete without mentioning my dog, Freddy, a mixture of dog and shepherd with a bright-looking, brown-and-white face who became so human to our family, we referred to him as Freddy Lowney, and he knew we did.

Freddy was courageous and never ran away from any dog, no matter how big or fierce, and he had the scars to prove it. He also had a bullet wound from a .22 caliber bullet that ricocheted when my brother, Hank, and I were plinking tin cans at the edge of town. Freddy followed us everywhere, even into the Rialto Theater when we'd sneak in the exit door. During the show, he'd sit quietly at our feet so he wouldn't attract the usher.

My main point about Freddy is that his death started my writing career. My fifth-grade teacher at Monroe Elementary School, Miss Kelly, told us to write a theme titled, "The Saddest Day of My Life." Well, I hadn't had a very long life at the time, but my saddest so far was the day Freddy was killed.

Hank and I were riding on the tailgate of a truck as it slowly headed up the Main Street grade. Freddy was running after the truck, barking. Suddenly I heard some painful yelps. We didn't see it happen, but obviously, Freddy ran under a wheel and was crushed. He limped to the gutter, and we jumped off the truck and rushed to him. I put his head in my lap and stroked him softly, calling his name over and over, somehow expecting him to get up and run around playfully as he had done so many times before, but it was not to be. Finally, he closed his big, brown eyes and went away.

It was freezing cold on one of those frigid January days so typical of a Butte winter. Hank and I took turns carrying Freddy to an empty lot near our house, but we couldn't bury him because the ground was frozen hard as concrete, so we tucked him under the snow to await the spring thaw.

I loved Freddy about as much as any little boy can love a dog, but I can't remember if,

Benny Crowley, Bobby Doull, Paul, Lenny Dawson and Freddy.

when the thaw came, we ever buried Freddy.

All this I wrote about in my theme. Miss Kelly graded my paper A- with the comment: "Excellent feeling and description, but poor grammar. You have talent and should continue writing."

Hardly a day goes by when some memory of Freddy doesn't surface in my thoughts. Like so many people who have bonded with a pet and consider the pet to be almost human, I, too, felt Freddy was almost human.

Just how human in my mind is illustrated by this tall tale I tell when any of my friends brag about their dogs: "My dog, Freddy, was practically human. One day he startled me. He told me he could talk. I gently patted his head and looked at him with a smile and said in a soft, patronizing tone: 'Freddy, it is a scientific fact of zoology that dogs can't talk. Admit you are lying.' "

There's a saying: "A dog is man's best friend." Also,
a child's best friend.

Kids who stole

In the growing-up experience, we kids knew that stealing was wrong, but those of us in the poorer neighborhoods of Butte felt that if we took something of small value from the well-off, it was okay—sort of. (My older brother, Hank, never used the word "steal"; he would say "annex.") And in my mind, there was another approval factor for stealing: Many of the older kids did it, and I looked up to them and I

The Butte-Silver Bow jail at Quartz and Alaska streets, presently not in use.
–Photo by W. Hinick

copied them. If an Eddy's Bakery van was left unattended, we'd open the back door and run off with pies and cakes. We'd climb on top of refrigerated boxcars and drop into the cooling department and toss out hunks of ice for our ice-boxes at home. At the P.O. News Stand store on Park Street, we'd read comic books at the magazine rack and sometimes we'd slip one or two books under our sweaters.

One painful embarrassment of my young life came at the Grand Silver store on Park Street where I was caught stealing several beans that fascinated me. Yes, beans – the Mexican jumping kind. I was ordered out of the store after a stern lecture, and I left meekly, hoping nobody I knew saw me.

To steal something to sell to the junkman, we'd climb on top of a building and strip away hunks of tar-covered lead that surrounded some of the pipe vents. One afternoon, we were caught, and the three of us—Hank, Benny Crowley, and I—were lodged in the Butte-Silver Bow jail facing Quartz Street—in the same spacious cell I had occupied two years later when I was 12. (See page 118.) At the time, Benny and I thought this episode was an exciting adventure, but the older head, Hank, was troubled and told us to get serious. We were released in a few hours, but the experience taught me most emphatically that stealing was not a game to play, but a wrong that came with a price.

These preceding infractions did not trouble my conscience for long, but there was an act of thievery that did, and I have thought about it off and on throughout the years, and I have wished that I could right this wrong. It happened in Butte High School. Hank and I had little or no money for school supplies, and if we did have the money, we didn't want to waste it buying tablets, paper, and notebooks—not when we could snitch these supplies from fellow students by raiding their lockers. We figured they were rich kids who could afford it. Of course, our reasoning was wrong, but something else was more wrong—the destruction of the trusting nature these kids had in their schoolmates. Eventually, the trusting ones used locks.

In a backward view of these petty acts of illegal mischief at Butte High School, I offer these comments – both light-hearted and serious: If any of you fellow students read this and recall that items were missing from your lockers, maybe I took them. Please don't call the cops. I'll pay you back. I'm sorry. This is my *mea culpa*.

If there is any person who at some time or other didn't steal anything of any kind, will that person please rise? Anybody? Nobody.

Lee – a remembrance with mixed feelings

A caring older sister is like a second mother.

T he oldest of my siblings was Lee, who was nine when I was born. To her, I was a real live doll to play with and care for. She dressed me and bathed me. The bath was usually in a large tub in the kitchen, and when it was bath time, my sister's girlfriends always seemed to be there. Even at this early age, I recall feeling annoyed that they stood around watching and giggling.

My sister took me on long walks – sometimes with her girl-friends. When we came to a curb, there was always this thing about swinging me over it while saying "wheeee." I have no idea why I should remember trivia like this, probably because they are some of my earliest memories.

Lee

Oddly enough, as much as I was the center of attention as the baby of the family, no one took a picture of me until I was five, and then it was only a small snapshot, with two front teeth missing, standing with my playmates, Bobby

73

Doull, Benny Crowley, and Lenny Dawson. I asked my older brother, Sam, why there were no baby pictures of me, and he brushed me off with, "We were out of film." (For five years?)

When I was six, my sister would take me downtown for treats at the American Candy Shop on Park Street, where we sat at a table in the mezzanine and usually had sodas. My sister told me many years later that it was in this little sweet shop that I broke her heart. Halfway through my soda I said, "I like all the treats you buy me, but I can't keep playing with the girls. I'm six and I want to be around my play-mates, Bobby, Benny, and Lenny. They are teasing me about playing with girls."

My sister looked crestfallen, but she didn't say anything. She was quiet the rest of the afternoon. I didn't realize how deeply she felt about being with me on these outings, and then suddenly without warning, our togetherness was cut off.

However, my sister did have a strong and lasting influence on me. She played our big upright piano and taught me how to find middle C, and to chord, and to play a few melodies. She talked about classical music and raved about opera. She took me to a matinee of I Pagliacci. At that time in my life, I found this opera to be a crushing bore and I tried to understand why my sister liked it so much. Here was a man in a clown suit singing in a foreign language a melody that was too classical and dull for my young ears. I tried to find something about it that I liked and I couldn't, but I didn't say anything to my sister because I respected her knowledge of things. However, I always remembered *I Pagliacci* and the man in the clown suit, and years later, when I became a dedicated fan of classical music, I finally appreciated the stirring aria from that opera – *Vesti La Jiuba.*

My sister studied Latin in Butte High School and shared her lessons with me. I can still remember a few sentences: *Ubi est puer?* Where is the boy? *Ubi est puella?* Where is the girl? It's one of those mysteries of remembrance that for so many years I can carry clear recollections of these Latin expressions, and yet today, words enter my mind for a moment and then skip away unrecorded. Sometimes I jokingly tell people that from my sister's reader, I know these two Latin sentences to perfection but that after all this time, not once have they ever come up in conversation. (And speaking of Latin, here are several expressions not in my sister's reader that I now use on occasion: *Quid pro quo.* Something for something. *Mea culpa.* My fault. *Pro bono.* Free. *Non sum qualis eram.* I'm not the person I used to be. *Ergo.* Therefore. *Sine qua non.* A necessity. *Cogito ergo sum.* I think, therefore I am.)

I saw little of my sister after she moved to San Mateo and soon married, bought a home, and established her roots as a Californian. It always bothered her that she was Jewish, possibly recalling some of the negative feelings and stinging remarks about Jews while growing up in Butte. There was always the undercurrent of negative attitude toward Jews. Being Jewish amounted to being a flawed person. I dealt with my Jewish descent by avoiding the subject around both my male and female friends. My sister chose another path. In California, she shed her Jewish birthright and became active in a Congregational Church. I always felt she did it for convenience and social reasons rather than out of any deep religious convictions.

As I matured, I examined my attitude and felt grateful for my Jewish heritage stretching back to the biblical Hebrews. I appreciated the substance and the richness of this historical civilization and the religious and musical culture, and I was proud that my bloodlines were a part of it.

I just couldn't feel at ease with my sister's Christianity. Though none of us children were raised in Judaism because of my father's insistence, but we did thrive in a Jewish atmosphere provided by our orthodox Jewish mother. As for me, a Jew is what I am – with or without religion – as it was with my antecedents stretching back in time for thousands of years; and I feel a security and a oneness with all Jewish people wherever on Earth they are.

When my sister died suddenly in San Mateo of a burst aneurysm, I was devastated and remorseful, but much of my emotion was in feeling sorry for myself and my own guilt. How unfair of her to die before I could show my appreciation and affection for her. Why can't people warn you that they are going to die so that you can make your peace with them instead of leaving you with guilt and so much unsaid and undone? I felt a stinging pain and a sadness that left my eyes wet. It was the end of my family. I alone was left standing. Out of a warm and active household of six going in so many directions, nothing remained but memories. First to leave was my father, then my mother, two brothers, and now my sister. But as do all living things, we must accept the contract with life – a beginning and an end. Ernest Dowson said it poetically:

> *They are not long, the weeping and the laughter,*
> *Love and desire and hate:*
> *I think they have no portion in us after*
> *We pass the gate.*
> *They are not long, the days of wine and roses:*
> *Out of a misty dream*
> *Our path emerges for a while, then closes*
> *Within a dream.*

At my sister's memorial service in the packed San Mateo Congregational Church, I had mixed feelings: proud of the outpouring of praise for her, and uncomfortable with the Protestant minister's references to Christ and Christianity – that is, not uncomfortable in a general sense, but only as these references applied specifically to my sister, the first-born of an orthodox Jewish mother.

On my flight back to Seattle, I felt melancholy and reflective. To ease my emptiness with the loss of my sister, I wrote – with my deepest feelings – these words in the format of a song lyric:

It's not fair
For you to go
Before I can say,
"I'm sorry."
You are gone,
And never
Can I tell you,
"I'm sorry."
Why is life so full of
Regrets and might-have-beens?
We just can't know
What lies ahead.
It's not fair
For you to go
Before I can say,
"I'm sorry."
I say it now
And somehow you'll know…
I'm sorry…I'm sorry…and
I love you.

Food from my mother's kitchen
What is us? Food is us.

As for the tasty and varied homemade foods I ate while growing up in Butte, how lucky I was to be born of immigrant parents and enjoy the eating delights of two cultures – Lithuanian-Jewish and American – and all prepared by the world's greatest cook, my mother.

Our family was aware of the typical American foods, which my mother called *chazzeri* (pig food) and urged us to avoid when away from home such as: ham, bacon, eggs, pancakes, beef, pork, hamburgers, hot dogs, donuts, chili, pie, and so on. But let me talk about some of the Jewish food my mother prepared for us in the same manner as in the home of her youth in a rural Lithuanian village near Kovno, where cooking was self-sufficient with most everything made at home, or as we say, from scratch.

From my mother's kitchen in Butte, here are (1) Jewish foods and (2) general foods:

JEWISH FOODS MADE AT HOME

Bagels	Donut-shaped bread dough, boiled and baked.
Blintzes	A crepe wrapper covering fillings of meats or cheese and then fried.
Borscht	Beet, (buriki) cold.
Borscht	Cabbage soup, sweet and sour.

Challah	Braided egg bread topped with poppy seeds.
Chicken soup	All chicken dishes started with a live chicken in our backyard.
Chicken soup	With matzo balls (knaidlach).
Coffee cake	A plain pastry topped with cinnamon.
Coffee cake	Filled with cinnamon-sprinkled cottage cheese.
Farfel	Tiny bits of baked dough or crumbled matzo.
Gefilte fish	Fish balls; a variety of fish, chopped and seasoned.
Gehakteh leber	Chopped liver.
Hamantaschen	Three-cornered pastries, generally filled with poppy seeds.
Helzel	Chicken neckskin, stuffed with a filling and sewn.
Herring	Chopped.
Herring	Marinated.
Kasha	A type of porridge usually made with buck wheat grouts.
Kishka	Cows' intestines with a filling and sewn.
Knishes	Dough with a filling of potatoes or chicken liver.
Kreplach	Similar to a wonton or ravioli.
Kugel	A baked pudding, usually made from potatoes or noodles.
Latkes	Potato pancakes.
Lokshen	Egg noodles, usually thick.

Matzo, fried	Matzo crackers are softened in water and then dipped in egg.
Pratkes	Stuffed cabbage rolls, sweet and sour.
Sponge cake	From matzo meal at Passover.
Strudel	Sheet-pastry of thin dough filled with fruits and nuts.
Tongue and brisket of beef	Pickled at home.
Tsimmes	A stew of carrots, sweet potatoes, and potato dumplings.

GENERAL FOODS MADE AT HOME

Bread

Cheesecake

Dill pickles

Donuts

Fudge, divinity, taffy, and panoche

Grape wine

Hamburger, ground at home

Horseradish

Ice cream

Jams and jellies

Pasties

Pies and cakes

Root beer

Sauerkraut
Tamale pie, chili, Spanish rice, carne
The usual variety of roasts, stews, soups, and breakfast foods

Of course, today, few people – Jewish or otherwise – would spend the time and energy to prepare food like my mother did – not in our busy society in which homemakers are often working – and especially when prepared, frozen, deli, and fast foods – and even eating out – are relatively inexpensive.

But my mother kept a kosher house, and cooking was her passion. She used culinary practices and recipes (unwritten) handed down by her mother and grandmother. I'll never find a wide variety of homemade food equal to my mother's, and I'm grateful that in those bygone years, my Jewish mother made the best, the tastiest, and the freshest food for her husband and her children.

We are what we eat, and considering the Earth's diverse population, what we eat depends upon who we are.

Ich shmek chazzer
(I smell pig)

There's an old saying that forbidden fruit tastes sweeter. Forbidden around our household in Butte by my orthodox Jewish mother was any product of the pig, which she referred to in Yiddish as a *chazzer*. Food eaten at home was acceptable, but any food eaten away from home, which my mother said wasn't kosher, was considered to be *chazzerai* (pig food) and was not to be eaten. This definitely included such items as hot dogs, hamburgers, chili, donuts, and of course, anything from the *chazzer*. My father, Jewish by genes but not by religion, was neutral on the whole subject.

One afternoon, while my mother was uptown shopping, my two brothers and I decided that this was our chance to eat the forbidden – bacon. We bought a small package at the grocer and fried it to a crisp. After we ate it, we carefully washed the pan and plates and opened all the windows to kill the scent. We didn't want any telltale smell to reach our mother's sensitive nose. What we didn't realize till later, however, was that little globules of bacon fat from the frying pan had a way of floating around the kitchen and landing on objects like curtains.

We were just closing the windows when my mother walked in with her arms loaded with packages. She set them down and a stern look flooded over her face. She placed her finger alongside her nose, took a few sniffs of the kitchen air and said in Yiddish: *Ah ha, ich shmek chazzer; du fresst chazzer un machst alles traif. Shvartz yor!* Translation: "Ah ha, I smell pig. You eat pig and make everything unclean. Black year!"

She was painfully annoyed and lectured us about eating bad gentile food and making her kosher dishes unclean. It was sort of a joke to me. I said, "Ma, it isn't such a big thing. Why get so upset?" My mother just responded, *Shvartz yor. Ich red tsu kinder – ich red tsu der vant.* Translation: "Black year. I talk to the children – I talk to the wall."

At that time, I never understood how important it was for my mother to keep a kosher house. She alone in our family of six struggled to keep her faith, her dietary laws, and her customs alive – separate kosher dishes; no meat and dairy on the table at the same time; cooking on Friday for the Sabbath; the candles on Friday evening and the special food observances on Passover and Yom Kippur. It was a losing battle for my mother. She had no help from the rest of us.

Later, as our family began to disperse, her projection of Judaism on her children was impossible. My oldest brother, Sam, and sister, Lee, moved to California. My other brother, Hank, and I went off to the University of Montana at Missoula. After my father died, my mother came to Missoula temporarily to keep house for us.

Never in my mother's lifetime did she eat the forbidden food, but in her final years she became more tolerant of food restrictions for her children. Just how tolerant was demonstrated by what she did in Missoula for my brother and me. Every Sunday, without fail, she proudly prepared freshly squeezed orange juice, eggs, toast, fried potatoes, and either ham, bacon, or pork sausages. Her love for us and the sacrifices she made to make us happy seemed to transcend everything else in life, including her faith. Religion was a large part of her life, but her children were a larger part.

P.S. I recall one incident, in Butte, in which my mother showed fascination and curiosity about the taste of bacon. Our Jewish neighbor, Maimie Halpern, spent a few days in the hospital, and after she came home, she phoned my mother and told her that she had eaten bacon. She said there were pieces on her food tray and she ate one. My mother was surprised and intrigued. She immediately phoned some of her Jewish friends, and with the enthusiasm of a news reporter breaking an exclusive story, she said: "I'll tell you something. In the hospital Maimie ate a piece of bacon," and then with emphasis, my mother delivered the punch line, "Maimie liked it!"

Mothers are motherly, but immigrant Jewish mothers are more so.

Love in grade one

It was in Miss Rosenstein's first-grade class at Monroe Elementary School that I fell in love with Marguerite McCauley, a cheerful little girl with a rosy complexion, who usually wore Scotch-plaid skirts. My friend, Raymond Deitch, was also fond of her. One time in class, Marguerite dropped her dainty small handkerchief. I picked it up and treasured it because it was hers and it had touched her body. Raymond offered me a dime for the handkerchief. To this day, I can't believe I let my need for such a small coin win out over my sentiment and tender affection for Marguerite. I sold this small piece of cloth, and I have always regretted it. The dime was soon gone. But the handkerchief that touched her would have been forever.

P.S. Marguerite, wherever you are, if you happen to read this, please call.

Odd ones in Butte

Like most small towns, Butte had its share of odd and eccentric characters known to most of the population. All of these people were lacking, either physically or mentally or both, and unfortunately, a lot of us kids, devoid of empathy, reacted to them with hurtful taunts just because they were different – or maybe, because of the way they were, we figured they expected it.

During my days in Butte, these were the ones I knew about:

Shoestring Annie wore bizarre clothing, was middle-aged, loud, large, and muscular, and as you might have guessed, sold shoestrings. Her usual beat was in front of churches and on the corner of Park and Main streets in the business district. When angered, she sometimes used her crutch as a weapon or a threat. We teased her now and then and would recite a jingle about her:

> *Shoestring Ann*
> *Doesn't give a damn*
> *She lifts up her dress*
> *And p_ _ _ like a man.*

A funny story that circulated about her – and I never knew whether it was fact or fiction – concerned Andy Davis, president of the First National Bank. Every day on his way to lunch, he'd give her 25 cents for shoe strings, but he'd never take them. One week, he was away for four days, and when he returned, Shoestring Annie approached him and said, "You owe me a dollar."

And then there was **Fat Annie**, who lived a block from our house. She had some type of malady, perhaps a type of palsy or St. Vitus's Dance – because she shook all the time and her speech came in slow hesitations and her eyes blinked continuously. Actually, we didn't say much to her other than to call her Fat Annie, but we did tease the guys who couldn't find favor with girls. "Hey, why don't you take out Fat Annie? She'll be grateful."

A well-known character in Butte was another Annie – **Nickel Annie**. She went about town repeatedly saying, "Five cents please," and sometimes, "If you don't have five cents, a penny will do." Nickel Annie never asked for more than five cents, and was always quiet and reserved as she walked the streets of Butte, a slightly built, forlorn figure, usually wearing a faded black dress. She stood on corners and knocked on doors, utter-

Nickel Annie as depicted by artist John McHatton.

ing her plaintive entreaty for five cents. On the copper miners' payday, she was certain to be seen at the pay office on Granite Street. After 45 years of begging, she died in a county home. The record showed her name was Margaret English, a well-educated woman from a prominent St. Louis family, and unlike some rumors, she was not wealthy. Her entire estate was a little more than 300 dollars in quarters, dimes, nickels, and pennies.

Joe was retarded, and we called him **Crazy Joe**. Sadly enough, we did torment him. We'd call him names to arouse and annoy him to a point at which he'd chase us and try to kick us. We'd always dodge his kicks, which made him angry, and in his frustration he'd spit at us and say "sonofabitch."

Another town oddity was **Joe No Legs**. The story goes that he lost his legs after he fell asleep on train tracks in a drunken stupor. He got around on a small, wooden, square board with wheels. Using both hands to hold two leather blocks, he'd strike the blocks against the ground for propulsion. We didn't tease him, but we did call him Joe No Legs to his face, and he didn't seem to mind – at least he didn't show it. With a touch of sick humor, one of the guys in our gang gave him a Christmas present every year – a pair of socks.

Probably our most glamorous character was **Flaming Maimie**, or as some called her, **The Painted Pony**. She was a woman of means who plastered her face with heavy, red makeup and wore gaudy clothes. She seemed sad and appeared to be searching for something as she walked up and down Park Street. She always carried large shopping bags, and rumor had it that she was a compulsive shoplifter and had been caught several times. We kids didn't say anything to Maimie. We just stared at her and smiled and wondered if the story we heard about her was true. People said that she lost her husband to a younger woman who plastered her face with heavy red makeup and wore gaudy clothes.

I still feel a bit of remorse about our unkind behavior toward these people. I suppose children are blunt in expressing their feelings and lack the maturity to realize how painful their remarks can be. In view of what I said and what I thought, let these words say I'm sorry to Shoestring Annie, Fat Annie, Nickel Annie, Crazy Joe, Joe No Legs, and Flaming Maimie.

We seem to be more comfortable with sameness
rather than with differences.

The girl and the scandal

In today's climate of sexual permissiveness and openness, this story would not be as explosive as it was years ago. The shock waves reverberated throughout Butte High School, and the city of Butte and threatened to cancel the football season for the Butte High team.

Let's call her Louisa. She was 18 and in her senior year – average looking, full-sized but not overweight; on the quiet side, a bit moody; and those close to her claimed there was a hint of deep feelings and yearnings locked inside. I knew her slightly but was never inspired to pursue a friendship with her.

I'm not certain how the story broke, but it did, and wide open. Several members of the football team, maybe five or six, were called to the principal's office. All of them admitted that after a party one night, they took turns having sex with Louisa, and according to her statement, they did not use force. Poor Louisa. The scandal was all over the city. The members of the team were severely reprimanded, and some of the faculty wanted them expelled, but the coach insisted they were not totally to blame, and the matter was dropped. As I recall, Louisa left school and returned the following year and graduated.

The entire episode was dismal and troubling, especially for Louisa, but this didn't stop some wise guys around Butte High from finding a humorous point in it. They suggested that Louisa should be awarded a football letter for making the team.

Butte's premier athlete – Milton Popovich

Milton Popovich ("Mia," "Milt," "Poppo") and I had two things in common: We were both Alpha Tau Omega fraternity brothers at the University of Montana in Missoula, and we both played football for Butte High School – but what we didn't have in common was this: Mia was a football star of the first magnitude, and I was a bench warmer on the third team.

Of all the athletic luminaries emerging from Butte High School, none shone more brightly than Mia, the pride of Butte people, especially his admiring immigrant Yugoslav parents. Although he was an outstanding performer on all of Butte High School's championship teams – football, basketball, and track – it was football that eventually brought him national fame.

The record of his athletic achievements in the thirties leaves little doubt that Mia was the best all-around athlete in the history of Montana sports.

In football, he seemed to be an unstoppable halfback, with dazzling long runs, sometimes the entire length of the field from kickoff; and adding to this were his versatile talents in passing, pass receiving, blocking, and coffin-corner punting. During his high school days, he made the All-State football team two years in a row, and at the end of 1999, he was named the best running back on the Butte High School All-Century Football Team. At the All-State High School Track Meet in Missoula, high-point man Milt drew comparisons to the legendary Jim Thorpe by winning the high hurdles, the low hurdles, and scoring points in the sprints, shot put, pole vault, the broad jump and discus..

After graduating from Butte High, Milton turned down offers from large prestigious universities, choosing to remain in his home state by enrolling at the University of Montana. It was at this relatively small school where he made football history by displaying the same skills from his high school days – running, passing, blocking, pass receiving, and punting. He was named an All-American, and for three consecutive years he was chosen All-Pacific Coast halfback. He played in the East-West Shrine Game and the College All-Star Game, and during his entire athletic career was inducted into four Sports Halls of Fame. In the year 2000, *Sports Illustrated* listed Milt as one of fifty all-time greatest athletes from Montana, citing his achievement as "All-American halfback at the University of Montana."

After leaving the University, Mia went on to play professional football for seven years, including five years with the NFL's Chicago Cardinals. Though successful as a professional, Milton always claimed that the best times of his athletic career were school sports, where he enjoyed the camaraderie of playing with his friends and classmates.

Popovich was an easy person to know. At the University of Montana, I frequently saw him around the ATO house where he was always pointed to with pride as our fraternity's candidate to the exclusive group of campus notables. For all his glory on the football field, he never put on airs. Those around him sensed he had a strong belief in his self-worth and that he knew exactly who he was – a natural-born athlete who could be one of the best in any sport he tried. Certainly, his accomplishments bore out this belief. He wasn't shy about expressing his honest feelings about others and himself, sometimes to the point of bluntness. In today's jargon, we would say of him, "He tells it like it is."

Milton not only earned fame for himself in the sports arenas, but emotionally, he took us along with him as dedicated fans. Competitive sports are made of conflict, aggression, and a struggle for victory; and as fans, we share these passions by identifying with our combatants. Mia was not alone in a Butte High School game when he took a ball from kickoff and raced 93 yards for a touchdown against Central High, or when in one game he scored five touchdowns. We felt his exhilaration. At basketball games in the Butte High gym, we cheered when he sank long-range baskets; and at the All-State Track Meet in Missoula, we enjoyed triumph when he won the gold by flying over the high and low hurdles as if they were only minor obstacles in his flight to the finish line. In college, he thrilled us when he zigzagged through the Oregon State football team for a 104-yard touchdown.

We all want our heroes. If we can't do it ourselves, then we reach out to those who can, especially if they are on our side. Milton Popovich made us feel good. He was on our side, and he gave us our Butte version of Jim Thorpe, Red Grange, and Wild Bill Kelly. From those of us from Montana: Thanks, Mia, for making our days.

Virginia Rule – did she know?

Some memories of small consequence never die, no matter how many years cover over them. As vividly as yesterday, I remember the unspoken affection I had for Virginia Rule, which was expressed more in symbolism than in reality.

It was my sophomore year at Butte High School, and the course was Physical Geography in a classroom of individual tables. Virginia sat opposite of me. We rarely spoke to each other, but I was totally aware of her – her reserved manner, her nice face with an almost Asian complexion, her large brown eyes, and a small mole on the upper part of her right cheek.

One day, the toe of my shoe accidentally touched the toe of her shoe. Suddenly, a warm rush of feeling flooded over me. I never moved my foot, and she didn't move hers either. All through the hour-long class, our feet were touching as if in an affectionate embrace. I wondered if she knew about this and if she experienced the same emotion as I did. She never said anything. Toward the end of my class my leg felt a bit stiff, but I didn't move it.

Every day in class our feet eventually found each other as though guided by radar. And as always, we never moved our feet away and we never spoke about it. I was shy and I knew she had a regular boyfriend.

As years went by, I never forgot Virginia Rule. In my mind, I can still see that classroom and her pleasant face and the tan leather shoes she wore most of the time.

It finally occurred to me that if Virginia ever came to a class reunion in Butte, I could fill a space in my memory bank that remained empty for so many years. Did she remember that Physical Geography class, and was she aware of our feet touching? At the reunion, I looked for her name on the list of those attending, but it wasn't there.

At the following reunion five years later at the War Bonnet Inn, I rushed to the bulletin board to read the list of those present. It was not listed, and then I looked at the list of passages. My meeting with Virginia Rule was not to be. Her name was there, and I was numb with regrets and loss.

Why did I not try to find her in the preceding years? I suppose I didn't think it was important at the time. But in a summing up and looking back at my life, it is now important. I couldn't accept it any other way: She must have been aware of my affection for her, and she must have known we were touching each other with feeling during all those classes.

Sometimes it would be helpful to have retrospect
ahead of time

Remember the yearbook

Call it what you will – the yearbook, the annual, the classbook; but by any name, it's what you get when you graduate from high school and college, and as the years roll by, the book is like vintage wine – it appreciates with age. The pages bring the past to life by recalling veiled memories.

Unfortunately, I have no yearbooks. All my materials from elementary school, high school, and the university were lost, including manuscripts, papers, photos, mementos, yearbooks, and annotated textbooks. These items were stored in a large cardboard box at my temporary residence in the Alpha Tau Omega fraternity house in Missoula while I was in San Francisco working a summer job. Little did I know that during my absence the financially-in-debt fraternity house was sold and all my stuff was thrown out. I have no records or cherished reminders of my school days. However, as an aid in doing this book, I have two yearbooks on loan to me from the Butte High School library.

Leafing through one of them – the 1937 yearbook – I was curious to know which student in that graduating class was the shining light – the one with the most citations for school activities and honors. I examined the pages of graduating seniors and was delighted to find that someone I knew and admired had the longest list – Betty Ann Graham.

There are twelve notations alongside her photo:

Director of Junior Play in Tournament
Declamation Winner
President of Athleta Club
Better English Club
Red Domino
Senior Play
National Honor Society
Annual Staff '37
Debate, '36
Bohunkus
State Little Theater Tournament, '35, '36', '37
President of Girls Organization

During our days of growth, such activities as these were the great moments and all-consuming events for expressing the potentials of our young lives, but in distant retrospect, they are merely pleasant memories covered with dust. If this sounds a bit dismal, there is the other side to it: What we were then is part of what we are now.

Moral of the story: Cherish your yearbook.

A boy discovers libido

Affection is a coal that must be cool'd
Else suffer'd it will set the heart on fire.
   – William Shakespeare

Billie

I was 14, a freshman at Butte High School, and one of the innocents. In the back seat of someone's car – probably Raymond's – I sat beside a girl I fancied, Billie Holliday. She snuggled close, and soon our lips met. It was my first kiss of any consequence, and I guess my thermostat went awry, because Billie touched my face and said for all to hear, "Paul, your face is like a red-hot stove. My, you are passionate." Passionate? What did this word mean? Thinking back on it, I believe that children from homes with well-educated parents were more informed and had larger vocabularies than us children from homes with immigrant, foreign-speaking parents.

I suppose I could have used a dictionary, but I didn't. The next day at school, a girl I knew walked by my locker and after the usual greetings, I said, "Billie said I was passionate. What does passionate mean?" She just giggled and hurried on. Now I was concerned.

Was it something dirty? I asked an upperclassman for the meaning of passionate. He told me, and I said, "So, that's what I am. I'll remember that."

In those times, young people were somewhat innocent about sex, and the code for sexual behavior was strict; the punishment for violating the code was a sort of social branding and ostracism – but for girls only. The boys were simply being naughty and "just being boys." The burden of upholding the standard fell to the girls.

Virginity-till-marriage was the accepted standard for females, and for males it was "get what you can whenever you can," and you're in luck if she lets you "go all the way." If word got around about a girl who "did it," she was marked and had plenty of date offers, but for all the wrong reasons.

As for me and the guys I knew during those school days, we never caused (or were able to cause) any girls to violate the prevailing standard. If a girl suddenly dropped out of school and went to another city, the suspicion was that she was either having a baby or found someone to perform an abortion.

Looking back on all this, I've never forgotten Billie. She awakened my male instincts, and I wouldn't mind if today I was still so biologically wired that a single kiss would make my face feel like a red-hot stove.

A poem to remember

Our first-grade teacher at Monroe Elementary School, Miss Rosenstein, recited a poem from our reader. I liked the poem and I said to myself, "All of my life, I will remember this poem. As the years go by, I'll keep saying it to myself so I'll never forget it." And that's what I did, and I never forgot it:

Come little leaves
Said the wind one day.
Come over the hills
With me and play.

Why did I want to remember this small verse? As one of my young friends would say in his pop vernacular: "I don't have a clue."

Sam – a good person, a good life

Of the four children in our family, my oldest brother, Sam, was far-and-away the most successful. He didn't finish high school and he didn't do anything special or achieve any particular status. He was just an ordinary person, and in my view, as normal as they come. In Butte, he was my authority figure, a role my father didn't do too well, and my mother was more interested in being motherly than in

Sam and Meyer

using discipline. It was Sam I looked up to, and it was Sam who set limitations for my behavior.

He went on in life to form a happy marriage, raise two children, and draw to himself a large number of friends. He made a good living working as a salesman for a food company owned by his wife's brother and mother. Sam could do things with his hands, especially plumbing, which he learned while working with my father, and he was always willing to help his friends and relatives with plumbing problems. Of Sam you could say in truth: Everyone liked him and he had not one detractor.

Sam was the mature one in our family. He was always older, even when he was younger, probably in part because in his early twenties, he started losing his hair and was treated as older, and in turn, he moved into the perception others had of him.

In Butte, two events involving Sam remain vivid in my mind, not that they were of much consequence, but because of the clear images they imprinted.

Event One: For some medical reason, tonsillectomies were *pro forma* at that time in Butte, and Sam had one. The only good part of this surgery was that during recuperation, patients were given milkshakes and ice cream. There was a puzzle about his operation. He came home with a black eye. We wondered how he could get a black eye from a tonsillectomy. Later, the mystery was solved. Before surgery, he had a fistfight with our next-door neighbor, Meyer Deitch – over a girl, I believe – but we didn't know for sure. It took only a day for Sam and Meyer to make up, but a lot longer for the eye to heal.

Event Two: I let my ego run away with me, and Sam put a limit to it. At that time in my life, my attitude was this: My male friends and my girlfriends and my high school activities are everything to me, and my family is just there to do for me: feed me, clothe me, and take care of me, but stay out of my way while I pursue my needs for sports, fun, and peer status.

It was the night of the big basketball game at the School of Mines gym. Butte High School was playing Christian Brothers High School, and I was to play in the preliminary game – Butte High's third team against theirs.

As I was getting ready for the big game, my mother asked me to do a small chore – bring in some coal from our shed. I said I couldn't because I had to go to the gym for the game. My attitude was: Why bother me with stuff like this? I'm playing before a packed house. Sam didn't like this attitude. He grabbed my basketball uniform and gave me an ultimatum: "You have plenty of time. Do what Ma asked you to do, or you don't get your uniform." I was furious. Who was he to do this to me? I'll never forgive him. I called him, "baldy." Angrily, I brought in the coal.

I stayed mad at Sam for a few days, but when I thought about it, I realized that I was acting like an uncaring egotist. Sam was right. This is my *mea culpa*.

The existence of a good person creates a ripple
effect that touches and enriches the lives of others.

A poem for Marjorie

Marjorie

I wasn't sure how to react to my affection for Marjorie Fennimore. I was 16; she was 17, and we met in a journalism class at Butte High School. Our teacher, Miss Williamson, a dowdy-groomed, middle-aged woman who wore a green eye shade in class, seemed more interested in the social lives of her students than in teaching journalism. If any boy or girl liked one another, they could share the same seat and hold hands or put their arms around each other's shoulders. I shared a seat with Marjorie, but I was too shy at that time to express my feelings for her. We worked together on *The Mountaineer* – our school paper, and one time, we went from class to class, making little speeches to promote the readership. I wrote a humor column for *The Mountaineer* called "Anonymous," and I'd always put my byline in code.

Being from the Westside and the daughter of a well-off accountant, Marjorie had a small coupe to drive. She would drive me to the outskirts of town and park, and we'd talk. Mostly I talked about football and my position as tackle on the third team. I didn't even try to kiss her. I don't know why. Maybe it was my shyness around girls or maybe some of it was something about the nature of the times.

During the time of my tender affection for Marjorie, I was working my way through *Romeo and Juliet* for an

English class project, and I came to admire Shakespeare's talent to say the profound in poetic language. I wanted to express my feelings for Marjorie with a hint of Shakespeare, and after some effort, I put together this note for her: *I see in you a person of beauty fashioned by angels, and a goodness that touches others with kindly regard and infinite soul; and if in these judgments I an dreaming, please do not awaken me.* I wrote another note reading: *Your mouth is a scarlet flower bursting with nectar – and I am a bee.*

At school, Marjorie would keep saying to me, "I'm going to embarrass you." Her girl friends would tell me, "Marjorie's going to embarrass you." I wasn't sure what that meant. One afternoon I found out. She came to my locker as I was putting my books away and kissed me full on the mouth. All her friends just giggled. What a nice surprise! I just blushed. I wasn't mature enough to do anything about Marjorie, so our friendship just drifted.

Later, I found out that she was involved with a policeman, whom I considered to be an older man – really old, about 25. She ended up marrying him.

The thoughts of Marjorie stay with me because I still remember my feelings for her and the poem I wrote for her one afternoon in study hall. I recited it to the young woman who is keying in this manuscript, and she urged me to include it in the book. It's not a very profound poem, no obscure symbolism, but passable for a sixteen-year-old. Did I give this poem to Marjorie, and if so, how did she react? How annoying – I don't remember – that image is lost, but not the poem.

Oh Were I Were

Oh, were I were a Shakespeare
With a magic pen to flow
Then I'd write countless volumes
Just to say, "I love you so."

Oh, were I were Miss Liberty
Who stands so firm and high,
Then I'd carry a torch as she does
Athrust up in the sky.

Oh, were I were Napoleon,
A conqueror strong and bold,
Gladly I'd freeze at Moscow
For a hand of yours to hold.

Oh, were I were a Caesar,
Or even play the part,
Then, dauntless I'd face hell, fire, and sword
In conquest for your heart.

Oh, were I were, Oh were I were.
Oh, were I were a famous man in history.
Then, I'd – ah, but what's the use in dreaming,
Because all I am is me.

You cannot say it wasn't love because love did not
last; but if for a time, love consumed your entire
being, then it was love at that time.

Dental braces

Dental braces have always been a status symbol in my mind, especially among females. That's because many Butte High School girls were from the well-to-do families on the Westside whose parents could afford braces for their children. These girls were classy: they had nice clothes, looked well-groomed and nourished, and their parents picked them up after school in Cadillacs. Now, whenever I see a female with braces, it attracts me.

I remember one of those schoolgirls, Polly. One time I asked Polly if she liked her braces and she gave a most peculiar answer. She said, "Whenever I get upset, I faintly hear music from my braces." She went on to explain, "My physics teacher, Mr. Bundy, told me that when I'm upset, my mouth creates acid and this interacts with the metal of my braces and forms sort of a baby crystal set, which is able to pick up weak signals from our local 50,000-watt station, KGIR."

"Does it bother you?" I wanted to know. She said, "I like the music, but the commercials bore me."

Was Polly making up this story about music from her braces? Was this some gag? I never knew. A friend of mine, an electrical engineer, said, "Theoretically, it's possible."

Fistfighting – Hollywood has it wrong

There were always fistfights in Butte, often near schools after classes or at dances and other social gatherings. Around Butte, fistfighting was routine. I believe it had something to do with the Irish immigrant influence and the ethnic mix of our city. When I vacationed one summer in Seattle while I was still attending Butte High School, I was puzzled about fistfighting. The fighting I saw in Butte as commonplace was missing in Seattle. At the time, I thought Seattle kids were all sissies, yet I was pleased with what I saw.

In my case, I tried to avoid fighting whenever possible. I didn't want to look like my older brother, Hank, with two front teeth knocked out, or have a scarred face or a smashed-in nose that never again would look the same. Although I had several small-kid fights of little consequence, nothing was very serious, and I had no injuries except for a few bloody noses.

This was to change on an occasion in which I couldn't avoid fighting, and it ended up a long-lasting, bloody battle that drained me completely and left me marked for many months.

Before I narrate this event, let me point out that Hollywood has a very sanitized impression of fistfighting. Unlike the films, it's not exciting, clean-cut, and harmless. It's not a pop in the head, and you're knocked out and soon you'll get up as good as new. It's destructive, fearful, sometimes lethal, and injures the one who delivers the blows as well as the one who receives them. Hitting the bony part of the head is like hitting a piece of plywood with your knuckles. And there's the sickening sound of the punch, sort of mushy, like striking a side of beef hanging in a butcher's locker; and of course, there's the blood, often crimson rivulets of it flowing from the nostrils or coming out of the mouth. Two movies that totally misrepresented the realism of fistfighting are oldies with John Wayne, *The Quiet Man* and *Donovan's Reef*.

My bloody battle came innocently enough on a chilly autumn night in front of the Terminal Drug Store on Park Street while I was talking to one of my high school classmates, Joe Riedinger. At the time I was 16 and in good physical shape from football training on Butte High School's third team.

Three grownups, obviously drunk, probably in their late twenties or early thirties, approached and passed some words with Joe, and Joe immediately ran off. Without any further words, a fist hit my temple, and I remember seeing flashes of light – call them stars if you will. If I had any fear, it was overcome by my anger. Why hit me? I didn't know these people. My only thought was: You can't hurt me and get away with it.

I immediately lunged at my assailant, my fists flying like a machine. At this point, two of his companions jumped in and a crowd began to gather, and I was fighting all three. At that moment, a thought of bravado flashed through my mind. Wow! Just like in the cowboy shows. One good guy is fighting all the bad guys – and winning. I should have been scared, but I wasn't. My adrenaline was pumping, and my heart was pounding. I was just mad. If these three hadn't been drunk, they would have slaughtered me, and I have no illusions about that. The punching and sparring went on for about 20 minutes.

The crowd kept gathering, but no one did anything but watch, so I hollered: "Will someone take two of these guys off me. Don't just stand there!"

Finally Pete, a friend of my brother Hank, and another fellow hauled two of the men off me. I continued to fight and I did something I thought I could never do, but consider the state I was in. I wanted this fight to end. I was dead tired and covered with blood, my own and theirs. My shirt was half-torn off, leaving my chest bare. I managed to get this man flat down on the sidewalk and, using his hair as a handle, I kept pounding his head against the cement. I was hoping he'd pass out so I could go home.

It didn't happen, but something else did, which left me scarred for months to come with an injury that changed colors almost daily, mixing purple, black, brown, blue, pink, amber, and a few in between. This man lifted his head to my chest and bit down on my left nipple. I screamed with pain.

At this moment, the sound of sirens wailed. I heard

later that someone in the crowd accidentally bumped against the drugstore window, and the store manager called the police. Pete lifted me off the sidewalk and ran me through the store and out the back door. Thank God, I was going home.

When I came home, my mother was asleep and I knew she'd worry, so I hid all my bloody clothing, washed myself and looked at my bruised nipple, put some iodine on it, and went to bed.

It was now morning, and my mother was going on and on between sobs – half Yiddish, half English. She found my bloody, torn clothes and was worried I was hurt, and she wanted to know why I was fighting. I said, "I couldn't help it, Ma. He hit me first."

Now I began to worry a bit. As Pete was taking me away at the end of the fight, I heard one of them say, "We'll get you later." I hoped in their drunken state they wouldn't remember, or that they would never run into me. I knew that if they were sober, I wouldn't have had a chance. They were fully grown men, probably copper miners, and fairly husky. Fortunately, I never saw them again.

During the following weeks, I was sort of a folk hero around Butte High School. One of my friends, Don McGarry, saw the fight and spread the word around. I mentioned to one of the girls that I was bitten on the nipple and soon giggling girls would come by my locker asking to see my injury, which I had no shyness in displaying. As the well-defined teeth marks in this injury began healing, the multicolors kept changing, and as I recall, it was several months before the discoloration was completely gone.

When I say that the one who delivers the blow suffers, too, let me explain. Both of my hands were swollen, appearing like round balls of raw meat covered with skin. My knuckles were barely visible. After all, these were hands that had repeatedly pounded against solid head bone. At school, I couldn't hold a pen or pencil to write the normal way, but somehow managed to scribble a bit.

But other than a mildly sore nipple, the most troublesome injury was a nodule that formed near the front of my jawbone. It was about the size of a BB, and whenever I shaved, I'd hit this spot and cut myself. I soon learned to avoid this area when shaving.

Again I say, Hollywood, you have it all wrong. Of the fights I have been in and those I've witnessed, I've never seen a clean surgical knockout blow like in the movies. When I see fistfighting in the films – sometimes comedic ones – the reality of the event doesn't ring true for me, and the make-believe illusion is shattered.

Looking back through the many years, I am surprised that the smallest details of this painful and exhausting experience are so vivid in my mind. I have described these events with total accuracy as I know them to be. Is it possible that an event of such high emotion and passion was able to make a strong and lasting imprint on my youthful brain? I think so.

This fistfight made me think about the measure of courage involved in such encounters. My brother, Hank, seemed to be fearless when it came to fighting, and unfortunately, he had two broken-out front teeth to show for it. I admired him for his courage, and this started me wondering about the whole concept of courage and street fighting. It takes courage to fistfight, because it can be dangerous, even lethal. In the case of my fight, courage was not the main issue. I was merely reacting to blinding anger without thinking about the consequences.

But what is courage? Nature provides all creatures with a survival instinct – fear. Without fear, we endanger survival. Yet in so many cases, if we act upon fear, we may risk being branded "yellow," or a coward. Then what is a brave person? Probably someone who feels fear and rises above it when the issue and purpose warrant it. Is it possible that people who are brave have a genetic high tolerance to fear, and the fearful people have just the opposite?

However you figure the balance between fear and courage, take heart that there are those who put courage in the forefront, for without these people, we would not have won our wars, or explored outer space, or built tall bridges and buildings, or extinguished threatening fires; or had our lives protected by those risking theirs.

Conflict and hazard are basic in all living creatures.
Ergo, it is dangerous to be alive.

Illogical "logic"

Sometimes we do things that have no logic or sense, and even though we know this, we keep on doing them. Maybe it's more comfortable that way. Here's a case: My sister, Lee, would never drink water from the bathroom basin at any of our residences in Butte, because she claimed that only the water in the kitchen was good to drink. Since our father was a plumber, my sister knew there was only one pipe bringing water into our house and that all the water was the same. But this fact didn't deter my sister, and she never gave up this belief. Many years later, I visited her in San Mateo and sure enough, there was no water glass in the bathroom, but there was one in the kitchen.

I shouldn't be amazed at my sister's belief because I, too, cast aside logic and fact. It had to do with a little kissing game we pre- and early-teens in Butte played at house parties. As I recall, there were "spin the bottle," "post office," and "wink-em." Obviously, all the games involved kissing, usually carried on with giggles, shyness, and a measure of innocence.

As for me, I had this thing about germs. There were pretty girls playing the game and there were the non-pretty girls. I believed that if I kissed a pretty girl, her germs wouldn't hurt me, but if it were a non-pretty girl, her germs were bad. The result? If I kissed a non-pretty girl, I would be careful not to swallow because I didn't want her bad germs in my body. What was the outcome of all this? Ordinarily, I don't write about unappetizing bodily functions, but I must tell you that if I didn't swallow after kissing a few non-pretty girls, I soon had a mouthful of saliva, and this was a problem. I couldn't talk with my mouth full, so I'd make an excuse to leave the room to purge.

And if you think that was illogical, I'll give you one more: After all these years, I still feel this way about kissing germs. It's simply a matter of emotion over fact, and if that's illogical, I don't care.

P.S. A few more examples of illogical rituals: At home, sometimes I listen at the top of the stairs to hear if the furnace downstairs is running, and, so I can hear better, I turn on the light. And in the same vein, a friend of mine puts on her glasses when using the phone to improve her hearing. This last one defies any modicum of reality: On Friday afternoons, my cleaning lady would remove the top blanket, fold it, and place it at the foot of the bed, because in her words: "It's always warmer on weekends."

Fundamentally, there may be no basis for anything.
    – Ashleigh Brilliant

Innocent boy goes to jail

Whenever I return to Butte for a high school reunion, I always drive by the jail on Quartz Street and look up at the barred windows. (Photo on page 70.) It was behind some of those windows where, at the age of 12, I was jailed for something I didn't do.

The manager of the Tripp and Dragstedt apartment building on South Main Street said that I was crawling along a second-story ledge to break into an apartment, but the total truth was that I was playing follow-the-leader with my friend, Raymond, and was trying to back him down. Unfortunately for me, Raymond, who could have verified my story, ran away when the husky manger rushed toward me, tugged on my legs and hauled me down. He took me into his apartment, locked the doors, and called the police. My protests of innocence fell on deaf ears. I hated that man and I was angry. I had a partially peeled orange in my pocket and in my frustration, I threw it hard against the wall and it smashed open. That didn't help matters any.

One of the worst parts of this troubling experience was passing through the center of town seated between two burly policemen in a large, black, four-door convertible Cadillac we all called the "Black Maria." I kept scrunching down so none of the townspeople could see me. What an embarrassment!

I was locked in a long, rectangular, rather spacious cell with two adult prisoners arrested for tearing down a wooden bridge and then hauling away the lumber. There was no youth detention facility in Butte, so kids were jailed with adults. The adult prisoners tried to cheer me, and to pass the time, I drew a hopscotch pattern with a small piece of chalk I had in my pocket and taught them how to play. I remember saying to them, "No, you can't step on lines."

Hours dragged on, and I soon learned the difference between being in a room with a door you can open, and being in a room you can't leave. I began to feel sorry for all the birds and animals in cages, and to this day, I will never own any creature that's caged, nor will I ever visit a zoo with cages.

The police called my parents, and after what seemed forever, my father finally arrived around sunset with Davey O'Connor, the juvenile probation officer. My father looked really good to me. The police took me into an office, lectured me, and returned a few items they had taken from my pockets.

All I could think of at the time was getting home to my mother, who would have the kettle steaming on the coal stove for making cocoa, and I'd sit at the bright oilcloth-covered kitchen table sipping cocoa from my Orphan Annie mug, feeling safe and secure. At that time in my life, the kitchen, with my mother in it and the kettle steaming on the stove, was the most comforting place on earth to be.

Following a threatening experience, how sweet is the ordinary routine of existence.

Judaism, European immigrants, racial feeling

In our household, my father objected to spending any money on religious education for his children; therefore, much of what I knew about Judaism was the customs practiced by my mother: baking and cooking on Friday so she wouldn't have to work on Saturday, the Sabbath holy day – the candles on Friday evening, and my mother with a shawl covering her head and waving her hands over the candles while softly uttering a prayer.

But mostly, the evidence of religion in our home was in the food culture: no *chazzer* (pig) or shellfish, no flesh of a wild animal, and only kosher meat from animals killed by the *shochet* (authorized killer). And there could be no *flayshedig* (meat) or *milchedig* (dairy) on the table at the same time. At Passover, no white flour was ever used in our home. Our bread was the traditional flat matzo crackers. The usual joke around our house at Passover time was a complaint from my father, who was Jewish by genes but not by faith. Like a stand-up comedian, he'd grumble to my mother: "I work hard all year and what happens? Come Passover, no bread in the house."

On two important Jewish holidays – Passover and Yom Kippur – my mother insisted that we children stay out of school. As for myself, I don't recall obeying my mother on this. I didn't want to miss school and I was sensitive about being Jewish and didn't want to be teased by my Christian friends, who projected an attitude that Jews were flawed people, something you don't brag about. For this attitude I could never find specific reasons on their part other than the prevailing historical accusation: "Jews killed Christ."

One time, my older brother, Sam, stayed out of Monroe Elementary School on Yom Kippur, and so did his good friend, Elmo Fortune. Sam had a good excuse for his absence. His teacher respected the sanctity of our holidays; however, she questioned Elmo's excuse. Elmo was black, or as we said in those days, "Negro." Sam and Elmo were fast friends, and Elmo was so fond of Sam that he wanted to be like him and be Jewish, too. Either he was serious about this or just wanted the day off from school. We never really knew. The teacher was a pleasant, understanding woman, and, according to Sam, she allowed Elmo's excuse with a knowing smile, apparently accepting Elmo's Jewishness, at least for the holidays.

And speaking of Elmo, a member of one of the few black families living in Butte, this brings up the subject of racial feelings and racial slurs in our city. Though Jews, Italians, and Yugoslavians came in for their share of name calling and teasing, blacks had the worst of it, some of it unintentional.

This made me wonder. Do names and terms carry inflammatory emotion and scorn if the people using them don't understand what they mean? As a child I learned the language the adults taught me. Words were symbols descriptive of things and actions. I didn't know that there was a racial intent when we called a certain nut a "nigger toe." It wasn't until much, much later that I learned that this food was called a Brazil nut. Though we knew the "N" word meant a black person, we – or at least myself – didn't associate scorn or slur when we said: "nigger heaven" for the very top of the balcony at our Rialto Theater, or before swimming: "The last one in the water is a nigger baby," or "There's a nigger in the woodpile." We kids were not mean-spirited little racists when we used these words. We were simply using the expressions given to us as part of our language in those days, and if anyone intended derogatory meanings for them, it would be based upon that person's full knowledge of the demeaning nature of those terms.

Jews had their share of racial slurs, some of them still used today. There's "Jew 'em down." (I take this expression in a light-hearted sense and it rarely offends me). And there's "long nose," and somewhere I heard this one: "The reason Jews have long noses is that air is free." And these names I constantly heard while growing up in Butte: *kike...Christ killer...sheeny...yid...ikie...izzy...hymie.*

Other ethnic groups were also targets of name calling. Around Butte, the Italians were called *wops ...dagos ...guineas*. The Yugoslavians were called *bohunks*. The Mexicans were called *greasers* and *spics*. The Irish were called *harps*, and because they were mostly Catholic – *mackerel snappers*. The English were called *limeys*. The

Chinese were called *chinks*. These negative appellations were made more hurtful by adding the word "dirty." For instance, "You dirty kike," or "You dirty wop."

During those times, feelings against Jews were mostly expressed in a condescending attitude, but sometimes were overt. The parents of one of the high school girls I dated preferred I not come to their home. We'd meet at the local soda fountain in the Grand Silver store. Her parents tried to talk her out of seeing me because I was a Jew. Another classmate, Ruby, said to me: "You're a handsome Jew." I interpreted this to mean being handsome makes up for the flaw of being Jewish.

I was annoyed and resentful toward my peers for having this "looking down" attitude toward Jews, as if there was something wrong with us. Why should I be made to feel bad about what I was? Should I resent my parents for being Jewish? – although many times when I'd suffer embarrassment over my Jewishness, I'd wish they weren't. Was I different from my childhood playmates and my high school peers? I was a good student, participated in all sports, and ran the high hurdles on the varsity track team. I was popular with girls and was vice-president of both the sophomore and junior classes, bodies of more then 400 students. Yet I avoided the subject of being Jewish, though I never denied it.

I remember sometimes at parties we'd engage in telling our descents. It went: "I'm Scotch-Irish" or "I'm English and German" or quite often "I'm Duke's Mixture." When this game started, I always found a reason to leave the room, usually for the bathroom.

It wasn't till later in Seattle, when I did publicity for a Queen Esther contest to raise money for the Talmud Torah Hebrew school, that I discovered the richness of Judaism: the Old Testament, the history, the literature, the music, the language, the traditions from biblical times. I said to myself, "Why am I turning my back on this?" I'm lucky to have this heritage despite sly, patronizing remarks from some gentiles. There was no reason for me to hide being Jewish as did some of my peers with clever evasions when they'd say they were Russian or Polish or German or Spanish, when the ultimate meaning was Russian Jew, Polish Jew, German Jew, and Spanish Jew. I criticized some of my Jewish friends for using a code when referring to Jews in the company of gentiles. They'd say M.O.T., meaning Member of Our Tribe.

In Butte, I grew accustomed to name calling and the feeling that somehow I was different from my Christian schoolmates and friends. All I could think of was – I'll show them. I'll make something of myself; and call it sublimation, if you will, but this feeling was for me a strong motivating force to gain some type of career recognition.

The litany around our household was: Don't ever marry a *goy* (gentile) even if you love each other. One reason: The first fight you have they'll call you a "Jew" or a "kike." In reality, it hasn't turned out that way in our family. My brother, Hank, and sister, Lee, married *goyim*, and so did five of my Jewish nephews, and the two divorces from these marriages were not because of racial conflicts.

There seems to be an erroneous belief among some that if you are not a religious Jew, you are not a Jew. Regardless of spiritual belief, one still has to have a descent, a genetic, biological makeup that comes about in any group living century after century in the same climate, using the same language, same customs and food sources.

With Butte a melting pot of ethnics from Europe swarming to this small town to work in the booming copper mines, what were the racial characteristics of the city? There were no programs to foster racial understanding, and "diversity" was only a word in the dictionary. Each of the foreign groups carried on with its own transplanted customs, religion, and language.

The Italians with their popular restaurants – Lydia's and the Rocky Mountain – dominated the northern part of town called Meaderville. In addition to restaurants, Italians were also successful in operating boarding houses, stores, markets, and bakeries.

Yugoslavians were an active and highly visible population in Butte. The Serbian Orthodox church was the scene of colorfully costumed traditional weddings and bazaars; and the city noted that Serbians – using a different calendar – observed Christmas on January 7. One of the most colorful events enjoyed by the entire city was the Croatian pre-Lenten carnival, Mesopost, a rousing celebration with music, dancing, feasting, and serenading, ending with the dramatic burning of a straw figure representing evil.

The Irish culture in Butte had a dominant presence in politics, law enforcement, saloon-keeping, and the Catholic religion. Their noisy shivarees, and even their wakes, were often festive, spirited events. Though some deny it, the Irish did have a reputation in Butte for fighting and drinking.

Butte had a sizeable population of Cornish miners from the Cornwall tin mines. They brought with them the pasty – a sort of boat-shaped, hand-held meat pie, still a popular food in Butte. In Cornwall, they were made with small dough handles (for holding with dirty hands) and taken down in the mines for lunch, and were sometimes referred to as the "tin miners' dinner." In Butte, the Cornish miners referred to them as "a letter from 'ome." Before I return from a trip to Butte I always stow a few pasties in my luggage. (See pasty story on page 162.)

Even though there were a certain amount of racial slurs tossed about and some isolated incidents of overt racial prejudice, on the whole, Butte was a friendly, help-your-neighbor, mountain-locked community. The racial feelings that existed were expressed more openly than in today's climate of the overly sensitive "politically correct." Racial epithets – and they existed – were accepted as merely a matter of expressing feeling, and I never heard of anyone in

Butte losing a job or being pilloried for racial jokes or racial slurs.

Even with differences among the ethnic groups, the basic friendliness of Butte acted as an adhesive holding our small community together with a fierce pride of "being from Butte." For some, there was no better place on earth to live, and though they traveled to other cities and countries, they always came back.

What is the city but the people?
– William Shakespeare

The Jones family – *mi casa es su casa*

What a remarkable, unusual family – the Jones family in Butte. If there were more like them, it would be a better world. But they were from another time, another culture, another ethos – a cheerful, loving, and industrious family who had fled the hard times in North Dakota.

They lived in a comfortable, small wooden house on Dakota Street. The family was headed by Ma (Josie) Jones, who always seemed to be seated in the same overstuffed chair, squinting at her crocheting. She had nine children, was separated, and did not divorce for many years because of her Catholic religion.

The Jones family conveyed a warm neighborliness typical of rural living in North Dakota, and this was apparent by the manner in which they welcomed drop-in company as if a sign on the door read, "Enter." Day or night, we just walked in. We never knocked, and the door was never locked. We were not treated as intruders, nor

Glenn

Marion

Joe

did we feel like intruders.

My brother, Hank, brought me to the Jones house for the first time, and it soon became my home away from home. Like a friendly clubhouse, we gathered there to talk with one another and with the Jones family when they were home, but mostly we played cards, usually three-handed pinochle, the cut-throat kind. I learned the game quickly, was good at it, and it almost became an addiction for me. If no one was at the Jones house – which was rare – a drop-in would wait around until someone came, and if three were there at the same time, pinochle was sure to follow.

Ma Jones rarely played cards. She crocheted and some-times would chatter away; and when the occasion arose, she would tell stories about life in North Dakota. Ma Jones was so typically and so delightfully homespun and down-to-earth, it was as if she was a caricature of herself, with glasses sliding down her nose as she peered over the top of them when talking and straight through them when crocheting. Her voice was small and somewhat squeaky and high-pitched, but it carried an air of authority when she had something to say. She held the family together and dispensed the rules and guidance, which all her children and drop-ins like me obeyed without question.

Besides Ma Jones, the other Joneses I came to know were Bob, the eldest, Joe, Phil, Glenn, and Marion. There was a small child around the house, Katie, whom I faintly remember. Except for Bob, all of them, including Ma Jones, seemed to look alike with the same-shaped, pudgy noses. Bob's nose was longer and straight, almost as if he weren't a Jones. He provided the main income for the family by selling eggs to homes all over Butte, delivering them in his Model-T Ford, which he drove with some difficulty because his leg was withered from polio. Joe was the talker in the family and the most open and friendly. Around Joe, you got the feeling that what was his, was yours, too. Phil was next, taller than the rest and more ambitious, and always finding small jobs after school to bring in extra money.

The one grown girl in the family was Marion, about 16 at that time. Poor girl, surrounded by males, she had little privacy and no female siblings in her age group to share her femininity with. She was cheerful and helpful and most of us wanted her favor, especially me. I had no idea she liked me, too, until one night we sat close while we listened to a radio drama. We started holding hands, and then, sitting silently in the dim light, we eventually had our arms around each other, and stayed that way until the radio program ended.

The other Jones I knew, I saved for last – Glenn, the only one who didn't fit the mold. He looked like a Jones, but in attitude, he had his own agenda and rebelled against the open-door policy. He grumbled about having no privacy and no place to study his homework. He resented our intrusion, but he was always overruled by Ma Jones. We called him "The Bull of the Woods." But, thinking about it, Glenn was right. How selfish of us kids to be so thoughtless about the need for this family to have space without invasion. However, Ma Jones seemed to like the activity of the young men in the house. It was company for her while she pursued her solitary business of crocheting.

It was a pleasant time, being part of the Jones family, and I, for one, learned lessons in neighborliness and friend-liness and how a family in hard economic times could make do for themselves and still share with others.

We kids were not unappreciative and we often brought gifts to the Jones house, and sometimes we'd climb into the Model-T and help Bob with his egg route. Eventually, we all drifted away: Our family moved to another part of Butte; some of the guys went off to out-of-town colleges, and one of the group joined the Navy.

Could a family exist today in the lifestyle of the Joneses? Perhaps, if the family lives in a small rural town in North Dakota that time has left untouched.

Regardless of how modern civilization becomes, no one has ever come up with a better plan than the family.

Columbia Gardens and the purpose of flowers

The crown jewel of our visually drab mining town was the Columbia Gardens, a pristine 68-acre basin of lush greenery two miles east of Butte. In the 1880s, this area was used as a picnic grounds, but in 1899, copper king William A. Clark bought the land and developed it into one of the nation's largest and most varied amusement parks, complete with a man-made lake, swimming beaches, a giant Ferris wheel, a roller coaster, a restaurant serving 400 customers, a large pavilion, flower gardens, and many other facilities and amenities.

Band concert at the Columbia Gardens.
-photo by Smithers

During the summer, we kids looked forward to Thursday, a day that Clark (who also owned the streetcar line) mandated free rides to and from the park and no entrance fee. The verdant Columbia Gardens was a welcome respite from life in the industrial atmosphere of a mining town, so it was with much regret that Butte people witnessed the closure of this financially troubled facility in 1972 following the collapse of the international copper market.

One of my clearest memories of the Columbia Gardens was watching the spirited event of pansy picking. There were fields of these carefully nurtured flowers, vibrant in the sunshine with a brilliant spectrum of colors. Could any field of flowers surpass the rich colorations of pansies? Not in my mind. The children – mostly girls – lined up at a starting mark, and at a signal, rushed into the garden and picked pansies, being careful not to uproot them; and at another signal, they hurried out of the field, holding the flowers in bags or in a slightly upturned dress. When the boys picked pansies, they always made it clear that they were getting these blossoms for their mother or for a girlfriend.

Now that I've mentioned flowers, let me digress from the main theme of this piece to comment on the purpose of flowers and the human attitude toward them. As I think back to the Columbia Gardens with its beautiful flowers, and then, today, as I watch shoppers carry armloads of them from supermarkets, I begin to wonder: What's the real

One of many floral designs at the Columbia Gardens.
-photo by Smithers

essence of a flower? Is it nothing more than an ephemeral organic object to delight the human senses? Flowers were here millions of years before humans came along. They are not here for humans, although in our anthropocentric attitude, we tend to think so. The purpose of a flower is its function in the reproductive cycle of the plant through hermaphrodite, male, or female sex organs. Bright, inviting colors and the sweet fragrance of flowers are intended for bugs and birds, the pollinators, and not humans. By picking flowers, humans intercept this cycle, as we also do with some other cycles in nature – for instance, a seedless orange. We really tricked nature on this one. The whole point of the delicious sweet pulp inside the orange is for the eventual reproduction of the plant through seeds, but we outwitted nature by scientifically developing this fruit without seeds, causing nature's intent to come up empty after all her miraculous effort.

Of course, all of this doesn't mean that you shouldn't enjoy flowers, but remember this: If you pick a flower, you may be cheating some insect out of dinner, and perhaps you are even thwarting the birth of another flower.

Ergo: When you praise the splendor of a flower, also praise its essence – parenthood.

Hank, my left-handed brother

During my elementary school years in Butte, my role model and mentor was my brother Hank, five years my senior. I followed him around and tried to do what he did, and copied his likes and dislikes, especially his food tastes. Later in life, when I lived in the freshmen dormitory at the University of Montana, I had to deprogram his food stereotypes or I'd have gone hungry. He wouldn't eat any-thing with mayonnaise in it, so that banned potato salad and most sandwiches; he wouldn't touch fruit mixed with vegetables, so Waldorf salad was out; he rebelled against eggs after he thought about where they came from; and to eat a beet, you'd have to tie him down and force one down his throat, because he said the little bit of liquid it oozed looked like blood.

Fortunately, I rid myself of all these dislikes, except for beets. To this day, I won't eat a beet. However, on a United Airlines flight after I

Paul and Hank in the summer heat.

136

had a gin-and-tonic, I bravely ate a beet, but I didn't feel good about it because, believe it or not, I felt I went against my brother, and I still won't eat beets. However, beets don't come up that often.

I always wanted to go where Hank went, and this annoyed him because he considered me a pest. He said I had no business hanging around with the big guys. One of the sharpest pains of my young life occurred under an arc light hanging on a corner of Aluminum and Iowa streets. He told me to stop following him and a few of his friends, but I wouldn't listen. He called me "fallycat," which in his jargon meant someone unwanted who follows. After repeated warnings, I wouldn't turn back, and then under the arc light I remember so well, he punched me in the belly and I doubled over and fell to the ground in pain while my brother and his friends marched off. That was the unkindest cut of all, and though I loved my brother, I never forgave him for that. And I always remember that bright arc light shining above my head as I lay there, crying and feeling very sorry for myself.

But years later, Hank proved to be my savior and protector. Fistfights around Butte were commonplace, and being Jewish was a magnet that attracted taunting and racial slurs and even aggression. Hank was always there to bail me out of fights if the kids were bigger or tougher than me. In my view, Hank was fearless. He'd fight anybody and he had a bridge for two missing front teeth to show for it.

My mother seemed to favor Hank because, as I saw it, he needed favoring. Compared to his siblings, he had more problems in dealing with life, and my mother always claimed his difficulties came from being left-handed. He'd always lose things, and his grooming was an eyesore. He'd never comb his hair, but simply swept his hand through the tangled mop on top of his head. Remember, in those days neatness was the standard and, unlike today, grunginess was not considered "cool." My mother would say to him in Yiddish: *Deine hor zet oys vi a vald*. Translation: "Your hair looks like a forest." Even as years went by, he continued his habits of disorder. His clothes and possessions were a jungle, and when he finally bought a car, the car took on the shabby appearance of the owner, and also would frequently break down for lack of care. The traffic tickets he accumulated went unpaid, as did his fines from the Butte Public Library for overdue books.

But Hank was one of the good guys. He was thoroughly likeable and attracted a wide circle of friends, especially among the underdogs, perhaps because they felt he was one of them. He had a sharp sense of humor and a talent for assigning names and descriptions to those around him. The names often took hold. He referred to Jews as "pork dodgers," and one of the spoiled rich kids in his class he labeled "Green Glasses." A lanky friend was "The Stork"; the "Gum Beater" was a talkative friend.

He was a nut about cleanliness, sometimes to the point

of two showers a day, and we'd know this by seeing tracks of wet footprints leading from the bathroom. For some reason, he had a speech deviation, a sort of peculiar, slow drawl. Where he picked it up is a mystery. In our home, he heard language in a standard cadence – Yiddish and English, and away from home, it was English. We joked about some of his pronunciations. Even as a teenager, he'd say, "Aws-twail-yuh" for Australia.

Hank loved school, almost to the point of addiction. Supporting himself by working in restaurants, he remained at the University of Montana for nearly eight years. It was as if he was hiding from life and used the campus as a sanctuary. When he finally left the university, he took with him degrees in law, economics, and education.

He ended up in California, where he taught school and studied for the California bar exam. He failed it twice, and according to his story, it was because the examiners couldn't read his writing, which usually looked like the markings of a chicken that stepped on an inkpad and then danced around on paper. Finally, using a typewriter, he passed the test.

He married, raised twin girls, practiced law in Pacifica, bought property, and even though successful to a point, he still would not comb his hair. Perhaps this was a symbol of his stubborn individuality. As usual, my mother would say that this trait was because he was left-handed.

My pre-teen years in Butte were molded more by Hank

than by my parents, and it wasn't until years later that I realized that some of the mold didn't fit, and I shed it. In looking back, I realized that all in all, Hank was a loyal friend and an important part of my emerging character and personality, and my affection for him is enduring.

In one of my early offbeat humor books, I used Hank as a subject for two humorous fables. Even though the fables are bizarre, I wrote them with kindly regard for my brother and for a point of humor, and his twin daughters understood that.

Fable One: My mother always thought Hank had problems because he was left-handed. That was not the reason. It was the unusual circumstances of his birth. By some freak of gestation, my mother carried Hank for 12 years, so you might say that when he was born, he was 12 years old. That wasn't all bad, because he was old enough to go right into the Boy Scouts without first being a cub. The only problem was that at Scout meetings he would fall down a lot because he hadn't yet learned to walk.

Fable Two: About 20 yards from our back fence on Iowa Street there was a hole leading to an abandoned copper-mine shaft. Hank was playing nearby and accidentally fell down the hole. It was his birthday, so we lowered a cake to him. Some brother. He didn't even tug on the rope to say thanks.

I always wanted to make it up to Hank for all the good things he did for me, but he was in California pursing his law practice and raising his children, and I was busy with my life in Seattle. At that time, siblings were not all that important to me because I was immersed in a life of work and play: I ambitiously pushed my career as a writer and publisher; and through my side job as a contract writer of a weekly humor panel for *The Seattle Times* I inherited all sorts of social opportunities and a certain amount of status, all of which filled my life.

Finally, I arrived at the point where I'd take the time to know my brother again and pay him back in some form or another for fighting my battles in Butte and for his all-around support during our university days. But with Hank, as with my sister, which I mentioned in this book, how was I to know sudden death would snatch them away before I could square accounts and allow me to purge my guilt for all I hadn't done for them? Ignoring doctor's warnings about his heart (he thought doctors were expensive nuisances), he collapsed and died while climbing stairs in a San Francisco building.

Thinking about the loss of these two siblings, Hank and Lee, I realized that sometimes we mourners indulge in a certain amount of selfishness. We feel sorry for the departed, but we think, "How unfair of you to leave my feelings so unrequited and make me so miserable because 'poor me,' I miss you and I need you and you leave me with lifelong guilt."

But at least this piece is my testimonial to Hank, my friend and older brother.

In spring, brothers are like leaves bound to the same branch, but in autumn, the leaves fall and scatter with the wind.

A built-in legacy of life

Since I have mentioned the loss of Hank and Lee in the preceding pieces, it is appropriate at this time to consider the feelings and mental states in losing family members, one after another, until at last, only one remains standing alone – and with remorse. If the reader finds the following too sentimental or disconcerting, the reader may turn to happier pages.

For all living forms, termination is the built-in legacy of inception – and when it comes to those close to us – we all face this transition in one way or another, depending upon the bonding and the relationship.

Realities fade away like morning mist, but memories live on, and memories put into words can live indefinitely. And so I put into words the memories of the Lowney family of Butte, Montana, a complete family of mother, father, and four children with all their passions, ambitions, conflicts – but memories only, since the players, except one, have left the stage.

The departures of my mother and my brother Sam were not sudden or unexpected as it was with my father and my two siblings, Hank and Lee, so in these cases that lingered on, there was time to make my peace.

My mother was terminally ill in a Seattle care center with metastasized cancer. The Army rushed me to Seattle from Alaska on emergency leave. Emotionally, I was prepared to show openly my affection for her, something I had never done in Montana because at that time, so many of Butte's bratty, so-called tough kids viewed being mushy with your mother as sissy stuff.

At the care center, the nurse said, "Come back tomorrow, I've just given her a shot. She's sleeping." My instincts were to wake her, but I was urged to wait. I wanted to put my arms around my frail mother and tell her I loved her and to hurry and get well.

This was not to be. A call came during the night from my sister-in-law telling me it was over. I was relieved for my mother's release from suffering, but I was frustrated and sad: I didn't tell her. I didn't tell her...I didn't tell her.... Now, I never can. To this day, I am still disturbed over being cheated of an emotional catharsis and an affectionate parting with my mother. At the time, the only way I could ease my nagging pain was to say over and over and over to myself: "She knew...she knew...she knew...."

The bitter lessons of remorse and guilt for not openly showing affection for my mother and for my brother, Hank, and my sister, Lee, would not go unheeded when it came to my brother, Sam, who like my mother, was terminally ill. I visited him in the care center as often as I could and was totally supportive – and this was my true feeling for him, although, in complete honesty, my behavior was partly to avoid bad feelings afterward.

I did what I could. I persuaded the care center to

give my brother a much-needed private room and I paid the extra charge for his privacy. I even offered to pay the expenses to send my brother and his wife, Edythe, to a clinic in Texas operated by O. Carl Simonton, M.D., who wrote a best seller, *Getting Well Again*, and reportedly was getting cancer remissions through positive thinking, meditation, visualization, and other alternate methods; but Sam and Edythe felt that all that could be done was being done in Seattle.

If the following words sound maudlin, then so be it. This time I was there just hours from passage time. I knew my brother was sinking, and in his room I couldn't endure his labored breathing, so I went to the hallway so my relatives could not see my tears. I came back in the room briefly and then I went home. That was the last night that Sam was alive. He was the best of the children in our family.

There's a saying that goes: "Treat people each day as though it were the last time you'd ever see them."

A job at Safeway

How many adults have marveled at how cheaply their time could be bought when they were juveniles?

Case in point: To make myself a June graduate rather than a January one, I took a semester off at Butte High School to earn money for college by working in a Safeway store on Harrison Avenue in the flat.

I was sort of a pooh-bah, but without influence or prestige – just someone who did most everything. I stocked shelves, unloaded 100-pound sacks of sugar and flour from a truck, swept floors, and wrapped groceries at the checkstand with paper and string. When I wasn't doing any of these jobs, I worked in the basement that had a ceiling so low it was impossible to stand erect – not unless I were a small child or a midget, all of which obliged me to move around in a crouched position like a primate. It was in this basement that I stacked cartons of canned goods and sacks of sugar and flour; and it was here that I sat at a table bagging white, brown, and powdered sugar and hunks of cheese that I cut from a wheel. After work, I did stretching exercises to regain my normal posture.

And making my job a little more difficult, I had to walk (or run) two miles to get to work – that is, if I couldn't hitch a ride.

How cheap was my time? Every Saturday at 6:00 p.m. I was paid eleven silver dollars taken from the register for a

48-hour week, six days a week. After three weeks, I got a raise – twelve dollars a week every Saturday. That comes to 25 cents an hour.

In Butte, the labor pool was large and jobs were scarce. The copper miners in the deep and dangerous mines – seeing their way around in the dark tunnels with carbide lamps fastened to their caps – were making about $4.00 a day for eight hours – that's 50 cents an hour.

Certainly, by current standards, wages were meager, but at that time, the cost of living was extremely low. How low? An average five-room house rented for $25 a month; a new Chevrolet coupe was $800; gasoline was 19 cents a gallon; a loaf of bread was around 12 cents; two dozen large eggs sold for 25 cents; a hot dog was a dime; and two pounds of cottage cheese was 15 cents.

Wishful thinking: Wouldn't it be great to have today's income with yesterday's prices?

A lesson from Hannah

After I lifted a bowl of wonton soup to my lips to catch the last bit of broth, it suddenly occurred to me that this is proper etiquette in a Japanese restaurant, but not the one I'm in now – Chinese. Ergo: What's acceptable in one place may not be in another. My mind then flashed back to my high school days in Butte when I suffered a painful embarrassment over table manners while having lunch in the spacious home of my best friend – Creighton Carlson. Creighton's mother, Hannah, served sandwiches, hot cocoa, and fruit. She was a slender, soft-spoken, genteel woman who was always kind to me, because as I saw it, she thought I was a good influence on Creighton because I was a serious student, determined to go places, and Creighton was aimless and lackadaisical with barely passing grades.

Before I get into the main point of this story of my embarrassment, allow me to digress a bit to talk about the Carlsons, my main contact with the manners and decorum of an upper-middle-class, American-born family. Hannah and Creighton lived in the shadow of the father, Ray, the owner of a small cigar store on Park and Main. I viewed him as an in-home dictator, the lord, master, and provider who projected an air of, "I know what's best for this family; and so for your own good, do things the way I tell you to." His rule, dispensed with stern authority, was not to be questioned.

But the real character of the family was Grandma Carlson, who behaved in an eccentric manner at the least hint of stress, and I use the word "eccentric" euphemistically. One afternoon when I was there, she went about the house saying over and over: "biddeley shiddeley...biddeley shiddeley...biddeley shiddeley...." Creighton, who merely tolerated his grandma, commented on this gibberish: "It's that damned chicken in the oven. She's cooking the dinner today and it's stressing her."

But back to my embarrassment. When my father drank tea or coffee, he usually poured the hot liquid into his saucer to cool off, and then drank from the saucer, possibly a practice that was acceptable in the Old Country. That's what I did at the table presided over by Hannah Carlson. I thought drinking from a saucer was the way it was done. How should I know otherwise? I also smacked my lips when chewing.

Thank God for Hannah. She corrected me on both infractions. At the time, I was annoyed and resentful toward her for making me feel so plebian. But her words lasted me a lifetime. This is what she said: "Paul, you are a nice, handsome boy and I don't mean to hurt your feelings, but it is not good manners to drink from a saucer; and also you should close your mouth when chewing so you won't smack your lips." Wow! I blushed. Why didn't my parents or my older siblings tell me otherwise?

Come to think of it, I've eaten with many high-income

adults who smack their lips when eating, and I can't figure an inoffensive way to correct them. Fortunately, none of them drink their coffee from a saucer.

P.S. Would it be tactless to show this story to my lip-smacking friends?

Are there some things your parents never taught you, but you wish they had?

My mother's mistake

I was eight years old and I had just come home from school. My mother met me at the door and said, "I had a phone call from Mrs. Halpern. She said she saw you in Doull's Drugstore sticking out your tongue at Mr. Doull. He's our neighbor and a good friend, and that was a mean thing to do. You're going to get it."

"But, Ma, let me explain."

"No buts. You're always with the buts. You stuck your tongue out at Mr. Doull. Mrs. Halpern saw you through the glass, plain as day. What more is there to say?"

She scolded me and then gave me a parting *patch in hinten* (a slap on the backside).

I said, "Are you all through, Ma? Do you feel better now that you got it out of your system?"

She said, "Go outside and play."

I said, "Ma, listen to me for a minute. On the way home from school, my stomach started to hurt. I went into the drugstore and told Mr. Doull I had a stomachache and was feeling sick, and he said, 'Let me see your tongue.'"

My mother was stunned. She started to cry and said, "What have I done? You're sick. I'm sorry; I didn't understand. Wait, I'll get you something."

I really didn't say the following words to my mother at the time, but if I knew then what I know now, this is what I would have said: "Stop crying, Ma. I want this to be an object lesson for you. What Mrs. Halpern saw was accurate, but its meaning was not the truth. Truth is not necessarily what you see with your eyes. Visual perception is merely sensory impression. Truth comes from interpreting and understanding that sensory impression. Without this approach to truth, you could end up disciplining an innocent eight-year-old kid with a stomachache."

Mother knows best – sometimes.

Six daughters and a black derby

Judge Jeremiah J. Lynch, an Irish immigrant from County Cork, was not only one of the most colorful and distinguished personages in Butte, but also was the father of a son named John and six daughters of which the two younger ones – Rosaleen and Esther – were beautiful colleens whom I dated at different times. The other daughters – Mary, Catherine, Anna, and Ellen – I noticed now and then as they swished around the Lynch household, always seeming in a hurry to go someplace.

The Judge arrived in America at the age of eighteen and after various manual jobs, came to Butte, where he worked for a while, and then went to the Kent School of Law in Chicago and graduated with honors. He returned to Butte, set up his practice, and became well known through his activities and leadership in community affairs, especially Irish-connected organizations, all of which led to his election as a state district judge.

When he strolled around Butte, you could spot him blocks away by his manner and attire. He had the air of an aloof aristocrat, yet he was open and approachable, as if he were two people: one, the father, husband, and story-telling Irishman and the other, the judge in the courtroom: a serious, no-nonsense, somewhat stern but fair dispenser of justice. The trademark of his attire was a hard, black derby hat that he always wore, even in the winter (a temptation for

us snowball throwers). His suits were dark and his shirts were white with a stiff collar.

The Judge was rarely there when I was in the Lynch home on West Silver Street, but the atmosphere seemed to hold his presence: a dutiful, lively Irish-Catholic family in awe and respectful of their distinguished patriarch. I was grateful to Judge Lynch and his wife, the former Margaret Kelly of Butte, for the existence of Rosaleen and Esther. Rosaleen was a typical Irish beauty with an almost saintly nature about her, and more than once I had the feeling that she entertained thoughts of entering the service of the Catholic church. Esther, whom I saw now and then after we ran into each other in Seattle, was more outgoing, demonstrative, and fun-loving.

Memories of the good Judge surfaced in me at the University of Montana by an Alpha Tau Omega fraternity brother, Mickey Walsh, also a total Irishman. At one time,

153

Mickey worked as a page in the U.S. House of Representatives, and he had a politician's lingo about him. According to Mickey, he was present in a Montana courtroom when Judge Lynch, as the plaintiff, challenged the legality of an election he lost for district judge, claiming gross fraudulence.

At the fraternity house, Mickey would do his impression of Judge Lynch pleading his case in the Gaelic-accented tongue of a true Irishman. The plea went something like this:

Your Honor, it seems that an honest man can't run for an office anymore without them stealing the votes away. Some of them vote two or three times. They go to the graveyard and take down the names from the tombstones. Even the dead men vote. They steal the votes away.

Later, the Judge was returned to office as district judge, where he remained until he retired in 1949. He died in 1961 at the age of 90.

The Montana Standard newspaper said of him: "He personified the rags-to-riches American dream of hard work and success…With his dignified demeanor, resonant Irish voice and ever-present black derby hat, he symbolized Butte's Irish-American community."

And my words about the Judge and Mrs. Lynch are: "Thanks for giving Butte a touch of class, and thanks especially for your two charming daughters, Rosaleen and Esther, who filled many of my days with cheer and delight."

Shoot-out at St. Joseph's

I've been in a Catholic church three times in my life: Once in St. Peter's as a tourist in Rome; another time in St. James in Seattle because the girl I was dating insisted; and the other time in St. Joseph's on Utah Street in Butte.

I didn't go into St. Joseph's by desire, but by necessity. I was having a water-pistol battle with Raymond, and I ran out of water, and rather than get squirted, I eluded Raymond and ducked into St. Joseph's. I noticed a vessel of water on a stone pedestal, so I filled my pistol and waited outside. Soon Raymond appeared. He believed my pistol was empty and he took his last feeble squirt at me, which fell short. I took careful aim and fired. The water drenched his head. He looked startled and said, "How come?" I answered: "Raymond, think of it as a religious experience you didn't get with your *bar mitzvah*. You were just baptized."

No particular reason for reporting this bit of trivia, except that it is true, and I wanted to save the memory. As for Raymond, he went on to become a pilot and a brigadier general in the U.S. Air Force.

Raymond

155

The fistfight that wasn't

Willard Larson was a troublemaker – always trying to get a fight started, even between friends like Paulie Dosen and me. He started passing notes in class – one to Paulie reading: "Lowney is not afraid of you," and one to me: "Dosen is not afraid of you." He passed a few more

Paulie

provocative notes, and soon he had a fight scheduled. I remember how careful Willard was to keep an eye on both of us combatants as we marched down the long stairway after our last class at Monroe Elementary School. He herded us to a vacant lot just off the alley south of the school.

A crowd gathered, and Paulie and I just stood there looking at each other, having no heart for this fight. Neither of us could back out for fear of being branded "yellow." You have to understand, around Butte, fights after school were a normal routine. We each threw some feeble punches, landed a few, and scrambled around a bit, posturing more than fighting. "Mix it up!" some of the guys hollered. Still, not much action from us.

Some of the bored spectators climbed on to the roof of

a vacant house so they could watch sitting down. One of the kids leaned against a wobbly brick chimney and it collapsed, sending bricks tumbling down the roof. A neighbor came out and said, "I'm calling the police."

The guys, bored with a dull fight, ran off, leaving Paulie and me standing there silently, looking at each other. Finally, I said, "Should we leave?" and Paulie said, "Yeah, let's." We shook hands, called the fight a draw, and ran off. We stayed friends for as long as I lived in Butte, and displaying a bit of gallantry, we both claimed that the other one had won the fight.

From then on, we were both careful to avoid Willard Larson.

Troublemakers make trouble for themselves.
— Æsop

The Unforgettables

Names. Names. Names. No special story in the following text; no philosophical or sociological conclusions or
insights – just names and brief comments about some of the
ones I knew at Butte High School and Butte Central High
School. As with all of us who have moved on in life and then
looked back, there are those with whom we shared our
youth, making memories too indelible to erase.

At another time – Butte High School

Lawrence "Spud" Buckley was small in stature but large in athletic ability and personality. He was president of the sophomore class and I was vice president, and he always kidded me about being in charge of vice.

Dorothy

Dorothy Floyd, a gracious creature whose parents owned a laundry, had a winning smile so incandescent she could light up night football. All the boys liked her, and though I went out with her a few times, it was a given that she'd end up marrying her on-again, off-again boyfriend, Ed Leipheimer, and that's what happened.

One of my favorite friends was **Ward O'Reilly**, from a large Catholic family, the father of which was a lifetime rail-roader for the Chicago, Milwaukee, and St. Paul. Ward was a Bing Crosby nut, and story has it that he was reprimanded by his mother for taking down a picture of Jesus and tacking up one of Bing Crosby.

How could I ever forget **Betty Rickerd**, who invited me to a Rainbow Girls dance at the Country Club and then stayed peeved at me for insisting we leave early because of my morning job at Safeway?

Booty

Howard "Booty" McIntyre, from a large family in a large house on Platinum Street, was a good friend bursting with energy and enthusiasm, a real class act, a high school basketball star who lifted my social standing whenever I was seen with him.

Hank Mueller lived in the Mueller Motel on Montana Street, a property owned by his family. He was a happy-go-lucky companion, always doing wild things, especially with automobiles, his pet craze. One bumpy, tortuous ride with him in his Chevy was enough – speeding up and down hills in the outskirts of Butte, making his own roads over rocks and tumbleweeds, down and up gullies.

My classmate, **Rune Hultman**, would never lack for food since his parents owned the popular Chequamegon Restaurant on North Main Street, where at that time a steak dinner was only 40 cents. Rune was a gregarious, likeable friend who always made me laugh even when he wasn't trying.

Rune

Why wouldn't I always remember **Martin Merkle**, a classmate, whose sister was the beautiful Miss Merkle, our eighth-grade teacher we all loved, especially the boys? (See page ???.)

Jiggs

Lindley "Jiggs" Barry was the only friend I had whose parents were divorced and who didn't live with either of them. He was placed in a boarding house run by a lady he called "Em," but quite often would visit his father, who lived in a hotel and had a drinking problem but was a generous man and often loaned Jiggs his Ford coupe. Jiggs was a talker and loved arguing, especially during the action in games of marbles. Whatever happened to Jiggs?

Some of my teachers from many years ago remain in my mind for no special reason other than that they were simply there, occupying a block of time in my life. Other teachers, however, left vivid imprints that last forever. Such a person was **Helen McGregor**, Butte High School's dramatics teacher. She was a pleasant woman dedicated to her work; a gentle soul with a love for her students so real and giving that we all felt it and reflected it back to her. Miss

Helen

McGregor was the only teacher I ever saw again after leaving high school. She came to our 45th class reunion at the Copper King Inn. We all gathered around her, pouring out bits of trivia and happenings from another time, hoping to rekindle a memory and possibly a remembrance of us as individuals. I'm not sure she remembered me, but she said she did. After all, during the passing years, there were so many of us, but only one Helen McGregor.

In addition to those mentioned here and in many of the stories in this book, there are other unforgettables whom I liked and admired, but who were not in my circle of close friends. But how could I ever forget them? **Al Bukvich, Al Brown, Sidney Hoar, Sue Babich, Alex Ducich, James Ballard, Polly Steele, Dick Raymond, Walt Milar, Harold Perkins, Sam Parker, Harry Finberg, Newton Russell, Fritz Divel, Margaret Melby, Thelma Melby, Howard Rickard, Danny Hayes,** and several others whom I forgot to remember.

You can live without pasties, but not as well

People who don't live in a mining town like Butte probably don't know about the pasty (pass-tee), and when they do hear of it, they call it pay-stee or pastry. (Ever notice how people feel more comfortable with the familiar? That's why my name sometime comes out Lowry instead of Lowney.) The pasty is a sort of hand-held meat pie that's as familiar in Butte as fish and chips in London and tacos in El Paso.

Pasties came to this country by way of immigrating Cornish miners. In Cornwall, women made them for the lunch pails of their men working in the tin mines. You'll generally find pasties wherever you find mining activity and wherever you find the English. Records indicate that the pasty was originated in A.D. 916 by itinerant Irish Catholic priests, who carried them on their missions as portable meals. Eventually, the pasties arrived in southern England.

Our neighbors from Cornwall, the Tretheways, made great pasties – plump, moist, and full of pieces of beef, potatoes, onions, carrots, and turnips. The crust was light and tasty. My mother asked Mrs. Tretheway for advice on preparing these nutritious delights, and Mrs. Tretheway said, "I'll

162

make a deal with you. My son, Northy, is having trouble with his second-grade reading, and if your son, Paul, will tutor him once in a while, I'll pay him a little, and I'll give you some pasties and show you how to make them Cornish style." Well, Northy was no problem, except for his chronic runny nose, and thanks to him and his mother, Cornish pasties came to our household.

My wonderful mother made pasties almost as good as Mrs. Tretheway's, but her dough was a lot heavier. In my biased opinion, my mother was the world's greatest cook when it came to making roasts, stews, soups, cabbage rolls, kreplach, and potato latkes, but her baking was heavy-handed. Everything was solid and dense – her bread, her biscuits, her sponge cake, her layer cakes, and even her bagels, size for size, would outweigh any normal bagel. I kidded my mother about her baking, and my mother, having a good sense of humor, accepted my light-hearted remarks with a knowing smile. (Around our crowded household, humor was a necessary ingredient for survival.) I'd say things like, "Ma, how can you afford to bake with the price of cement so high?" Or: "Great! You're making a lemon pie with graham cracker crust. When it's done, I'll help you lift it out of the oven."

We'd have pasties once a week, except during the Passover week, when white flour for the dough was a no-no in Jewish orthodoxy. As a pasty junkie, I'd get withdrawal symptoms during that week, so my mother came up with an idea: For the crust, why not use kosher matzo meal instead of the forbidden white flour? And that's what she did – matzo meal pasties. My mother claimed we had the only Cornish-Jewish pasties in the world. One time, after I finished two pasties in a row, my mother said, "Were they all right?" With a straight face and a serious tone, I answered, "I'll let you know in two hours. It takes that long to get to my lower intestines." She just smiled. As I said before, my mother had a sense of humor.

You can live without pasties, but not as well.

A phone call to Maimie

I was nearby when my mother phoned Maimie Halpern, her best friend in Butte. Early in the conversation, I heard her say in Yiddish, *Maimie, du machts tsimmes?* Translation: "Maimie, are you making carrot stew?" There was a pause, and then my mother said, *Ich denk ich shmek tsimmes.* "I think I smell *tsimmes*." After she hung up, I said, "Ma, you really are a character. You can't smell over a telephone." She just muttered, *Ich denk ich shmek tsimmes.*

Think about this: If, at the time, Maimie was actually making *tsimmes*, this event would have been an unusual coincidence or some sort of olfactory telepathy. But as it turned out, Maimie was not cooking *tsimmes* and hadn't for weeks. She was washing dishes.

Your reality may not be what it seems to be, but "what it seems to be" is your reality if you believe it.

165

A vision of June Ralph

June Ralph was absolutely without a doubt the most beautiful girl in Butte High School out of a student body of more than 1,000. In my mind, she was a vision to behold with her facial symmetry and her dark-brown hair nearly touching her shoulders and her creamy skin with just the right amount of makeup to accent her classic features. To my eyes, nothing in the world was more beautiful than June Ralph – not Helen of Troy, Delilah, or even the Taj Mahal. But then again, I suppose it's much easier to be beautiful when you're only 16.

Getting a date with her was something beyond my expectations. Like so many of the girls of her group from the tony Westside with parents of means, they usually dated the boys in their own economic and social class. There were a few exceptions, mostly in the case of star athletes. As for me, the son of a plumber and someone from across the tracks (and there were tracks at Iron Street for the trains carrying copper ore from Butte to the Anaconda smelter), I managed now and then to be invited to some of the Westsiders activities at the Country Club. The largest economic and social gap in Butte was between the managers and office workers of the Anaconda Copper Mining Company, the Montana Power Company, and the banks on one side, and the copper miners and other laborers on the other side.

The rumor was floating around school that June Ralph didn't have a date for the big Junior Prom. Well, as the vice-president of the junior class, the dance was a must for me. Could it be that June Ralph would go with me? I approached her in the hallway, and the answer was yes. An excitement flooded over me that was both good and bad. I was glad, but I was also concerned. June Ralph with me? Would I be up to her expectations? Since I was not from her social set of Westsiders with expensive houses, I was not totally comfortable with the date.

The night before the prom, I tossed and turned and I don't think I slept much, but at the age of 17, lack of sleep didn't bother me.

At the prom with June, I wasn't certain how to behave with her. I didn't want to show I was overly impressed and be a pat of warm butter in her presence, so I went the other way – a bit forward and a bit sarcastic – truly an example of overcompensation. In return, June was pleasant enough, but I could see she was annoyed.

Though I wanted to behave differently, it seemed my mood and deportment were locked into the behavior I brought to the evening. Something would have to change, or the adventure of the prom would be lost and so would any closeness with June Ralph.

Fortunately, something did happen that lifted me out of my frame of mind, and it was due to my classmate, Gene Kelly, and a crazy, offbeat joke he told me earlier in the day

– a joke that sent both of us into fits of laughter like two drunks caught up in a contagious laughing spell because everything to them seemed funny. Later, I'll tell the joke.

At the prom, Gene Kelly walked toward us, and just seeing him surfaced the joke in my mind, and I began chuckling. He told it again, and we were both howling before he got to the punch line. June was mildly amused, but was unaware of what had happened earlier in the day between Gene and me.

That laughing spell opened the whole evening for me, and I became less defensive and unconcerned about impressing June. The prom and the after-prom stopover at the Red Rooster drive-in went exceptionally well. At her doorstep, June thanked me for a nice time and kissed me goodnight. I was happy, but for me, June was not to be. Shortly after the prom she made up with her regular Westside boyfriend, and I never dated her again.

What was the joke Gene Kelly told me? *A drunk walked into a bar and took a live lobster out of a paper bag and said to the bartender: "Here's a live lobster for you." The bartender said, "Gee, thanks. I must take him for dinner," and the drunk said, "No, don't do that. He's had his dinner. Take him to a movie." *

My memories of the prom – the music, the dancing, the little paper programs, a tableau of colorful long dresses and dark suits with ties – have nearly faded from my mind, but not the vision of June. That remains clear and precious. If

I were to meet her today – and no matter what the years had wrought – I would, in my mind, see her as the beautiful June Ralph of yesteryear, my date for the Junior Prom.

A footnote to this joke: Years later, the newspaper supplement, *Parade*, ran a feature on me and my humor using jokes and gags from the galleys of my then-forthcoming hardback, *The Best in Offbeat Humor* (Peter Pauper Press), and in a biographical note, the editors quoted the lobster joke as the bit of hilarity that ignited my interest in humor writing.

"A thing of beauty is a joy forever" – *especially at the Junior Prom.*

Halloween the wrong way

Many of us children in Butte never understood the true meaning of Halloween or why or how this observance came about. We believed that Halloween was open season for doing destructive things to the grownups, their homes, and to public property. At that time, I had never heard of the expression "trick or treat." For the victims of our destruction, the condition of "treat" was not a choice we offered. We did, however, hear of something still done today: soaping windows. But soaping was sissy stuff. When we resorted to something that mild, we'd use candle wax – much harder to remove.

Butte was a tough city, and we kids living in the poorer neighborhoods were supposed to do tough things, especially on Halloween, and what amazed my child brain was that the police were out to get us. I felt they had no right to chase us. Wasn't it Halloween and weren't we supposed to celebrate it by doing bad things?

What sort of bad things? Here are just a few, and I'm sorry to say in retrospect that I was part of the gang doing them: We'd tie ropes around the doorknobs of front and back doors and anchor down the rope, usually to a fence, and then ring the bell or knock. Sometimes we'd climb on roofs and pour water – or even a can full of urine – down any chimney issuing smoke. One of our favorites was removing someone's gate, shinnying up a pole, and untying the line that lowered the arc lights for bulb-changing, and then we'd fasten the gate to the line and hoist the gate high in the air. Another nasty was finding garbage cans full to the top and leaning them against someone's front door and then ringing the bell. There was an assortment of other hurtful acts, such as breaking streetlights, pushing down fences, greasing doorknobs, and knocking over garbage cans. Our biggest fear through all this was being caught by the spoilsport cops, and our cry was always the same as we ran away to hide: "Jiggers, the cops!"

In other parts of town, vandalism was often more widespread and serious. The kids in these neighborhoods came together in gangs for Halloween, as though they waited 364 days for this special night to vent their emotions and indulge in the high jinks of senseless destruction. For instance: Sheds, fences, wagons, and cars were toppled or demolished; windows were smashed; horses or cows were tied to front doors or placed in schools and churches; brakes were released on ore and coal cars standing on a grade, which caused them to roll, often crashing; streetcar tracks were smeared with axle grease, allowing them to run out of control; gunnysacks were stuffed into smoking chimneys, driving the fumes into the living quarters of homes; and there were many, many other harmful acts done in the name of Halloween. Is it any wonder that extra city police and sheriff deputies were called to duty on this troublesome night?

"Trick or treat?" At that time, there was no such expression in Butte.

What troubles me in a backward view is the belief that we weren't doing anything wrong. It was the accepted game of Halloween: Do the dirty tricks and then get away with them. If kids today are as vacant-headed as we were when we saw no wrong in these senseless acts of vandalism, I then conclude the sometimes-forgotten obvious: Children must be taught and told "what is right" and "what is wrong" and "what is good" and "what is bad," because, left on their own, they have no genetic ethical monitors. In my view, mothers and fathers are on the right track in parenting if they accept the premise that children innately don't know anything about anything, since they come into this world empty, like a computer without software and input data. They must be given a culture, not dispense one.

I'll never forget Mr. Thomas

I'll never forget Mr. Thomas.

Our Troop 2 Scoutmaster found odd jobs for us needy kids so we could earn money for a week at the Ruby Creek Scout Camp north of Butte. One of my buddies, Mike Chakarun, and I were given a job digging dandelions from the lawn of Mr. Thomas, who was the treasurer of the Montana Power Company. I can't remember our pay, but it was probably about 40 cents an hour.

After we finished the work, Mr. Thomas hired me to water his lawn every day while he was on vacation. For three days I rode my bicycle a couple miles up the hill to his house on West Platinum Street and faithfully watered his lawn. Then, some fun things came up in my young life, and I didn't have time for the watering. I never went back to the lawn.

One day a call came from Mr. Thomas, so I pedaled over to his house. I knew I was in trouble. He showed me his brown-parched lawn, thirsting for water. Only some of the hardy dandelions (which Mike and I missed) survived the unusually hot Butte summer.

He paid me for the days I watered and then he said, "Young fella, here's some advice: As you go through life, keep your word. It makes you a person. When you keep your word, you're like a rock; when you don't keep your word, you're like a shadow." I told him I was sorry, and then I rode off on my bicycle with his words of admonition seared into my brain where they were to remain the rest of my life.

Eight years passed and I was home on summer vacation from the university at Missoula, and I was looking for a job to earn money for school in the fall.

An idea occurred to me. I called the Montana Power Company and asked Mr. Thomas's secretary if I could have a short meeting with her boss, and she arranged it.

Mr. Thomas didn't recognize the twelve-year-old boy who was now 20, so I said, "Maybe you remember. I'm the one who let your lawn burn when I didn't water it, and you gave me some good advice on keeping my word, and I've never forgotten it." I then went on to say I needed temporary work to earn money for college.

He seemed impressed with my attitude. He made a few phone calls, and then told me to report to the power company shop on Montana Street, where I would be taught how to cut pipe with an electric saw. I thanked him most warmly.

Before I left his office, he puffed on his pipe a few times and said, "You know, thinking back on that lawn years ago—the grass burned but the dandelions withstood the heat and drought. Makes you wonder. Why not put in a yard full of weeds instead of grass?"

I'll never forget Mr. Thomas.

A good lesson learned should be a good lesson taught.

Games we played

There were five movie theaters in Butte: *Rialto, Ansonia, American, Liberty*, and *Broadway*. We kids usually avoided the adult love films, which we called "mush," and so after we'd seen all the suitable movies, what did we do for recreation, especially in the evening? There weren't any television, videos, or electronic games, but there was radio, and about radio, I've always wondered, what do you look at while you're listening to the radio? Maybe nothing. In a car, you look at the road.

So in the absence of canned entertainment, we did things that kids probably don't do today, but would be better off if they did. Sans any equipment, we played outdoor games, usually after dinner at nightfall under any street corner that had an arc light shining. Not only were our games good exercise, but they taught us how to interact with one another and how to be competitive. Mostly, we played, "Lamppost Coming In," "Run Sheep Run," "Kick the Can," and sometimes "Hide and Seek." If there weren't enough guys to fill out the sides, we'd let the girls play, too. In the winter, our favorite game without equipment, other than snowball fights, was "Fox and Geese," in which we competed by running on paths we pressed into the snow.

This leads me to a point I've wondered about for years. We hollered an expression when we wanted to terminate a game and allow those "out," or away from the starting point, to come in "free." It sounded like "Olly, olly outsin free." My research on the origin of this expression came up empty. A book titled *Encyclopedia of Word and Phrase Origins* stated that word sleuths couldn't find a definite answer. I've always felt that "Olly, olly outsin free" was merely a childish contraction of "All that's out is in free." Anyone have any contrary views on this?

Lorraine Anderson, the spirited one

During my elementary school days, we lived on Main Street south of Iron Street in a neighborhood with many children in my age group, which meant that after dinner there were enough of us to play games in the street. Lorraine Anderson was the only girl we'd let play with us boys. Other girls called her a "tomboy." In part, she was, but in other parts, she was a delicious, rosy-cheeked, spirited female who made my pulse beat faster when I was around her, but I'd never let her know that. From our viewpoint, she was merely a girl whom we tolerated to fill out the sides of our games.

She had plenty to say and was never intimidated by the guys. Her trademark was her everlasting gum chewing and the sweet odor of spearmint gum. Like so many kids our age, Lorraine and I never seemed to talk each other in normal tones. Mostly we hollered, especially when arguing about the games or most anything else that came up.

I saw Lorraine's mother a few times through the window of her small house on Fremont Street near Main Street. She was divorced, young, and pretty, and I had the feeling that she endured indifference from some of her close neighbors because there was usually a man named Boyer around her house, and sometimes it appeared he stayed overnight, which, during a time of tight moral standards, violated the code of behavior.

Lorraine was oblivious to all this and remained the most sought-after and admired girl in our band of kids. One time during a game, when we were both on the same side, hiding in the dark, I kissed her on the lips. The kiss was pleasant and sensual and had the aroma of spearmint gum.

Miss Merkle – a teacher the boys liked to love

Our eighth-grade teacher, Miss Merkle, was the most beautiful teacher at Monroe Elementary School. All the boys in her eighth-grade class had crushes on her. She was about 24 years old and was more modern than the rest of our teachers, and also less strict. We could never figure out why some of the grownup men around Butte didn't pursue and marry her. Of course, if they did, she could no longer teach, because at that time only single women were allowed to hold teaching jobs.

My affection for her was expressed by just looking at her and enjoying her pretty face and her easy manner of teaching. She was fun, but she also demanded and established discipline. On weekends, Miss Merkle ushered at the Rialto Theater, where her shapely figure complemented her white and gold usherette uniform. We kids were always glad to see her at the theater.

At that time, I was 13, and I will tell you truthfully that if Miss Merkle had asked me to come home with her and spend the night in her bedroom, I would have jumped at the chance. I would have been in hog heaven. I think many of the male students in my class felt that way, too.

If this fantasy were reality and considered wrong in the eyes of society, I think you'd have to define it as politically wrong, not biologically wrong. And by this I mean that the rules of conduct are political, but feelings of physical sensuality are biological. I am aware that feelings cannot be the only standard of behavior and that for good reasons, there are political standards by way of laws. But in this hypothetical case, if Miss Merkle – like in the present-day Mary Letourneau incident – were to be put in prison for her actions, I would have, at that time, asked to share her cell – at least for a while.

The Boy Scouts – a paradigm for living

Why are my memories of my distant past so clear? I can remember the names of all my grade-school teachers, my two scoutmasters, and many long-ago conversations verbatim; but today it's hard to remember whom I met last week or what I had for dinner two days ago. Somewhere I read that when you are growing up, your brain has more storage space and an abundant supply of the powerful alpha waves, which make strong imprints on the brain.

Thinking back on my two scoutmasters – Kenny Eisler and Mr. Coates (it was always Mr. Coates; I never heard a first name) – I realized that scouting was a significant part of my life. It gave me a value system, which in some ways I still carry today: Be helpful, do good things, lead a productive life, and develop skills in camping, craftsmanship, first aid, and personal health.

Scouting taught me many lessons for a productive direction for my life, lessons that I didn't always get at home; and scouting helped me curb the mischievous behavior I often copied from older kids, some of whom ended up in the reformatory in Miles City.

After I left scouting, I had a hard time accepting money for little jobs I did for my neighbors. The Boy Scout concept of doing a good deed and refusing payment was deeply ingrained in me, but I finally learned that there is a difference between accepting money for substantial work and refusing money for a small effort now and then.

My strongest memories of scouting were taking my tests for merit badges and scout camp. At one of my class reunions in Butte, I made an effort to find the camp. I remembered it was north, bordering on Ruby Creek. I wanted to see it and relive some of my experiences at camp: the unheated open-front cabins that chilled us at night…the smell of pine trees…our swimming in the cold mountain water of Ruby Creek…the reveille bugle call for wake up, and taps in the evening…and most of all, the nightly campfire where we sat around on logs listening to ghost stories to a background of a crackling fire – stories like the spooky "Monkey's Paw," and then, half-scared, wandering off in the dark using flash-lights to find our cabins.

In my search, I never found the camp. Perhaps the years had swept it away, but not the remembrance – that remains forever.

Passing St. Joe's

When I walked by St. Joseph's Grade School on my way to Monroe Elementary School, some of the kids in front of St. Joe's called me names like "Jew" and "Christkiller." It was one of my first encounters with racial slurs. I told them that the Jews didn't kill Christ – the Romans did, and they said that the Jews made the Romans do it, and I said, "Don't blame me; I wasn't there, and as far as I know, none of my relatives were either."

I told my mother about the name calling, and she said in her Old Country accent, "If they call you a 'Jew,' just say, 'proudofit,'" and that's what I said, "proudofit." It wasn't till later that I learned that "proudofit" was not one word, but a whole sentence: "proud of it."

Thinking about it, I realized that a lot of Yiddish-accented sentences sound like one word. For instance, there is *Vehyagoin*? Where are you going? And there is *Housebyyew*? How is it by you? And also: *Huhvieya*? How are you? And *Heysadonder*. Hey, sit down there.

Many years later, when I returned to Butte for a high school reunion, I looked for St. Joe's on Second Avenue. It was torn down, and workers nearby were pouring concrete for a foundation. I commented to the foreman nearby, "I see you are putting up a new building." He looked rather bored and said, "My company has a strict policy. We never put up an old one." So much for St. Joe's and being Jewish.

The haircut game

I hated getting haircuts (and I still do) so I'd let my hair grow until it was falling in my face and creeping down the back of my neck; and at a time when short hair was the uniform of the day, the difference between me before and after a cut was such a contrast, that one time my science teacher at Butte High, Mr. Bundy, remarked, "Anyone know why Paul is absent, and who is that new boy sitting at his desk?"

Mostly, I disliked lounging around the crowded, stuffy, single-chair barber shop on Arizona Street awaiting my turn, so I arranged a little game with Frank, my barber. I'd walk in and say, "I'd like an estimate." Frank, a jolly, stocky man in his fifties, would look at my head, front and back, and give me a quote, and then I'd say, "I have to get two more bids. If you are low, I'll be back." And then, amid puzzled looks from waiting customers, I'd march out.

In about 20 minutes, I'd come back and announce for all to hear, "Okay, you were low."

Only the barber and I knew the game: My first appearance in the shop was the signal to put me in line for the chair.

The Red Rooster – lost in time

How could I ever forget Butte's Red Rooster restaurant and drive-in on Harrison Avenue in the flat where I worked summer weekends as a curb-hopper while still in high school? Most vivid in my mind is a romantic song piped to the parking lot that frequently played as I stood behind a neon sign attired in a red and black outfit waiting for cars to pull up. The song, which is heard today now and then, is, *I Only Have Eyes For You*, or as we called it in those days, *The Iceman Song* (change "eyes" to "ice" and you have a virtual homonym). Whenever I hear this song it puts me in a mellow mood, recalling those warm summer nights watching pairs of my fellow students in their party clothes coming and going.

My one irritation, in addition to the neon sign blinking in my eyes, was that on Saturday nights I had to wait on a fellow student who would honk for service from his new Ford coupe, seated beside a girl I also dated. But that minor pique was not what stirs my present nostalgia of the Red Rooster. What does, is the sound of that dreamy ballad: *I Only Have Eyes For You.*

Thinking back, I've wondered about the Red Rooster and about the owners, a hard working, hands-on couple, Mr. and Mrs. Venable. When I was in Butte four years ago, the Red Rooster was no longer a drive-in, but an upscale supper club. While writing this book, I wanted to know more about this place of so many of my pleasant recollections, both as an employee and a customer. My phone call to Butte was answered by a woman who said that for some unexplained reason Red Rooster calls came to her, usually about three calls a month. She told me that the Venables sold the place years ago and moved to an area near Yellowstone Park, and that later the Red Rooster was torn down and replaced with a commercial building.

How inconsiderate of changing times to sweep away this mecca for teenagers where lasting memories were born – where young lives searched for good times, love, and romantic adventures.

Anymore, does anything endure, other than the Grand Canyon, Niagara Falls, and the great pyramids in Egypt?

Are memories better than the original?

The woman upstairs

I remember our basement flat in the three-story frame building at 713 South Wyoming Street. As a little fellow, less than 10, I believe, I can still see in my mind Kate Pogreba, because I had strong feelings of affection for her. She lived above us and was frequently around our flat. She was pretty and her only flaw was a crooked front tooth. From my view, she was an older woman, but in thinking back, she was probably about 24.

She was my idol, and I always was on my good behavior in her presence. Sometimes she would breast-feed her infant, Donnie, while she was talking with my mother, and this stirred warm feelings in my youthful mind.

Her husband was another "older" person, probably about 26, a boilermaker for the railroad. His nickname was Skin, and I was jealous of him because he had Kate.

We moved away from Wyoming Street, but I never forgot Kate. As the years passed, I always wondered about her. Word drifted back to me about the Pogreba family from my sister Lee, who kept in touch. Kate still lived in Butte, but Skin died and her oldest son, Junior, was killed in the military. I never knew what happened to Donnie. Lee mentioned that Kate was ailing, and I wanted to see her. At my last class reunion in Butte, in 1995, I found her name in the phone directory, and I called. I just had to let her know how I felt when I lived on Wyoming Street, so I told her that I had this feeling of affection for her, and I'm glad I said it because these were my last words to her on this subject. She chuckled and brushed aside my remark.

She gave me directions to her house, and I drove around in my rental car, failing to find her street. It was close to the time of our class banquet, so I gave up. I called her from my hotel and said I'd try to see her on my next trip to Butte.

Looking back, this was another of the many regrets in my life. I flew home to Seattle the next day, and it was only a matter of a few months later that my sister called from California to tell me that my beautiful lady, Kate Pogreba, was gone. How I wished I could do it over and see her one last time. What I have left of Kate is a vivid memory of a little boy who, in a child's way, "loved" an older woman who lived upstairs.

Feelings of affection are based on emotion, not logic.

Virginia, the keeper of Oz

"A good book is the precious lifeblood of a master spirit,
embalmed and treasured up on purpose to a life beyond life."
– John Milton

I read every Oz book I could get. My parents couldn't afford to buy the books, and the library had a waiting list, but fortunately, I made friends with a pleasant girl, Virginia Horton, who lived on South Main Street across from our house. Her uncle and guardian, Floyd Fluent, was a successful lawyer of means, and Virginia had nearly all of L. Frank Baum's Oz

Virginia

books. My attitude toward Virginia was rather neutral because at the time, I was intrigued by a spirited, indifferent girl, Lorraine Anderson (See page 177). I admit I was a bit deceitful in my friendly attitude and the attention I showed Virginia because she was kind enough to lend me her Oz books. One after another I read: The Wonderful Wizard of Oz, The Marvelous Land of Oz, Dorothy and the Wizard of Oz, The Tin Woodsman of Oz, The Road to Oz, The Emerald City of Oz, Glinda of Oz, The Scarecrow of Oz, The Patchwork Girl of Oz, and probably a few others.

After I finished the last of her *Oz* books, I sort of faded from Virginia's view. I had no strong motivation to see her, and at the time, I was too insensitive to realize how this might hurt her.

Later, as I looked back on my actions, I did feel a bit of guilt, and it bothered me. But as fate would have it, I was able to vent this guilt.

Many years later in Seattle, a voice on the phone said, "Paul, you may remember me as Virginia Horton. I now live in Seattle and my married name is (I forgot) and I am now a grandmother, and you may remember that in Butte, you borrowed all my *Oz* books, and when you finished the last one, you never called me anymore, and you hurt my feelings."

Well, what a surprise! I was glad to hear from her, and what a break – a chance to rid myself of a bit of stored guilt in my memory bank of things I did wrong.

She accepted my apology with kindness, and then to cap it off, I said, "Why don't you come over to my house?" and she said, "I would, Paul, but I don't trust you." We both laughed and then we went into small talk about our lives and people in Butte at a bygone time.

Book lovers never go to bed alone.
– Anon.

Two ropes: one for play; one for homicide

Some memories of my childhood in Butte are pleasant and warm like a glow from a hearth on a frosty night, but other memories are cold and disturbing – and even more disturbing in present retrospect when my feelings are richer in empathy.

We kids had little knowledge of Butte's past, and it wasn't until later that we learned that the Chicago, Milwaukee & St. Paul railroad trestle we used for play was the same trestle used years earlier for a brutal lynching.

This is the story as I now know it: In the middle of the night, six masked vigilantes drove to a rooming house on North Wyoming Street where they found Frank Little's room, broke down the door, pulled him from his bed in his underwear, beat him, and then hustled him off to a waiting car for transport to the trestle in the southern outskirts of Butte. Evidence indicated that for a part of the trip he was tethered and dragged.

Frank Little

At the trestle, they slipped a rope around his neck, pinned a warning sign to his underwear, and then threw him off and left him dangling a few feet from

191

the ground until he was found the next morning. The numbers on the sign (shown below) were an Old West vigilante signature for warning outlaws, and denote a grave 3 feet wide, 7 feet long, and 77 inches deep. The letters at the bottom are the first letter of the last name of those being warned. The circle around the Ⓛ obviously indicated Little's demise.

This happened during World War I, when Little – a small man, 38, with one eye and a gimpy leg – was a labor union leader activist and fiery speaker for the highly controversial, revolutionary I.W.W. (Industrial Workers of the World), an organization that sought to overthrow capitalism by using propaganda, boycotts, and strikes.

Our play at this trestle also involved a rope. We'd fasten one end to a railroad tie, and then, holding the other end, we'd swing out over the downward-sloping

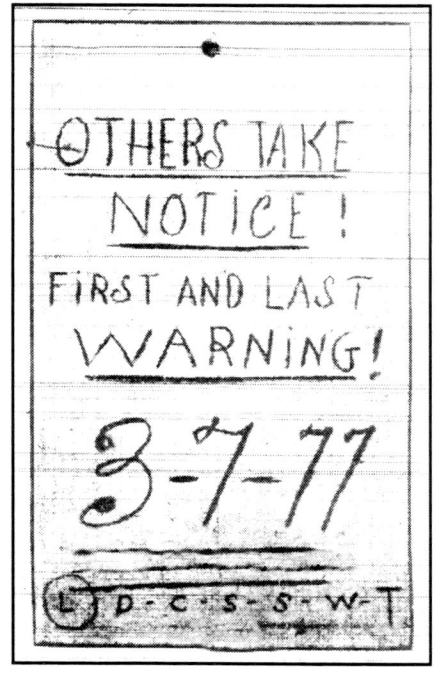

ground, pretending to be Tarzan flying through the jungle on vines. Sometimes, we'd let go of the rope and fall into the dirt, but mostly we'd swing back to the starting point.

After an adult told us that Frank Little was lynched at this very trestle, the impact of this horror did not fully register on me, and I continued to play there. I thought of it as an impersonal, violent act that grownups did, like something in a movie, but looking back at this tragedy, I now feel remorseful that such human-to-human cruelty could exist. I wondered what was going through the minds of those homicidal men as they overpowered this poor soul struggling for his life and then forced him from this execution scaffold. Were they paid killers carrying out an assignment, or were they impassioned believers whose hatred and anger smothered their reason and pity?

The obvious question arises: Did they ever find the guilty ones? No. In an atmosphere of fear and murderous threats, there were leads and rumors, but no arrests. The crime is unsolved. Some historians point out that because of the strong feelings of antipathy toward the I.W.W. and Little – especially by the powerful and dominant anti-labor-union Anaconda Copper Mining Company – Butte authorities did not try as hard as they should have to find the six assassins. (See page 206.) Little, unmarried, was not from Butte, but his followers buried him there, with a headstone reading: *1879 – 1917. Frank Little, slain by capitalist interests for organizing and inspiring his fellow men.*

Adding to the sinister and murky episode of the lynching is this item from the book editor's "Introduction" to the 1999 publication of *Nightmare Town: Stories* by the famous detective/mystery writer, Dashiell Hammett. The item reads: "Working for Pinkerton as a strikebreaker against the Industrial Workers of the World in Butte, Montana, Hammett was offered five thousand dollars to kill union agitator Frank Little. After Hammett bitterly refused, Little was lynched in a crime ascribed to vigilantes."

The players and the stage are gone – swept away by time: Frank Little, the vigilantes, and their supporters – vanished; the railroad trestle and tracks – demolished; but the story remains forever: A nightmarish tale of violence that blemishes Montana history.

Christmas in Butte; the human need for spirituality

Though I lived in a Jewish home with an orthodox Jewish mother, Christmas for me in Butte was an irresistible, contagious spirit that swept through our small mining town and through my consciousness, making everything seem different, especially on Christmas Eve – the night air, the sky, the stars in the sky, even the sound of my footsteps crushing the winter snow. It mattered not that the theme of Christmas wasn't the faith of our family, and that my people did not accept Jesus as the Messiah. Still, Christmas was Christmas, a national and spiritual holiday of enormous impact. In Butte – with its large population of devout Christians, especially the Irish Catholics – Christmas was total, deep, and meaningful, engulfing the entire city with a feeling of goodwill and joy. You couldn't be raised in Butte and not sense it.

The Christmas season awareness in Butte that inoculated my being was the sensation that during this period, all existence was unique and special, and this awareness was to remain with me for many, many years. I poignantly felt it much later as a soldier in the barren, windswept Aleutian Islands as I walked alone one night down a snowy path towards my Quonset hut. It was Christmas Eve and a clear night and the world and the heavens took on a kind of majesty – everything was changed; even the silence of the lonely night had a different sound, and the stars were brighter, and the chilly night air seemed warm and friendly as if it held some transcendental, unspoken message just for me. Was there any reality to all this? Reality? Do not our minds create our own realities?

In passing years, my feeling for Christmas slowly eroded, and today, I simply notice Christmas rather than participate in it, but whatever the belief, or non-belief, the event of Christmas in this nation is more than an activity of faith; it is a ubiquitous national drama touching all our lives.

Of course, today, all the trappings of the Christmas observance are much as they were in yesteryear, but in Butte at that time, it was more so. On Christmas Eve, the city closed down. After sunset, no store, restaurant, or theater remained open. Activities were in the churches and in the homes, and on Christmas Day, anyone's home was everybody's home as people went from one to another to see the trees, the gifts, and to drink a cup of cheer and enjoy offerings of food.

My mother and father remained aloof from the Christmas season, but the spirit of holiday came to us children primarily through school Christmas programs and our many neighborhood Christian friends and schoolmates. My sister, Lee, who seemed to resent being Jewish, was the most active in holiday festivities, even to the point of wanting to bring a small tree into our home and calling it a Chanukah bush, but my mother was unimpressed and told my sister to leave the tree in the forest where it belonged. Chanukah, a secular eight-day observance by Jews around Christmastime and not a Jewish holiday, was not as exaggerated at that time as it is today; and it is my belief that the present increased emphasis on Chanukah by both Jews and gentiles alike is a way of giving Jewish people – especially children – something to celebrate as a reaction to the Christmas festivities surrounding them.

When I was little, my older siblings told me about Santa Claus, and for a few years I hung my stocking. On Christmas Day I found things such as a wind-up train, dominoes, and tinker toys, but then I made the mistake of announcing that there was no Santa Claus. As Christmas approached, I said I was wrong, "There *is* a Santa Claus." It was too late for belief, but I hung my stocking anyway. My father and two brothers responded with humor, but with disappointment for me: In the morning, I found my stocking filled with clothes pins, pieces of coal, and an orange.

Comparing Christmas then and now, the most significant difference is the role of public schools. What went on in Butte public schools at that time would give fits to those today who interpret the First Amendment as banning prayer or any religious activity in the classroom. During my time in grade school and high school, the First Amendment was not an issue. Other Jewish children and I participated in Christmas school programs without complaint or protest. We copied the words of *Silent Night, O, Little Town of*

Bethlehem, and *O, Come All Ye Faithful* from the chalkboard and sang them in class. I knew that these activities were not part of my mother's beliefs or any of my Jewish friends, so I just considered them an education in the Christian religion.

This makes me wonder why, today, some people think the sky is falling if a few moments are set aside in classrooms for silent prayer of one's choice. A bit of prayer could be a helpful tonic to balance the deluge of harmful trash dumped into youthful minds by television, motion pictures, and videos.

But why God in school or any other place? Let's try this: In the thousands of cultures throughout the world – past, present, industrial, and primitive – a spiritual belief in a higher being was and is always present by whatever name – God, Allah, Zeus, Baal, Ra. Dr. William Howells noted in his book, *The Heathens*: "...societies without religion have never been found."

It is logical to assume that with the evolution of the intelligent, thinking brain, humans were able to search for a supreme being, a god, to explain the mysteries of life and the universe, and to provide dogmas for the conduct of their lives, and to allay fears. The great mind of Albert Einstein posited, "It was the experience of mystery – even if mixed with fear – that engendered religion."

In the thousands of faith groups throughout the world, it can be assumed that many conflict with one another, so which among these groups are true and which are not? It doesn't matter. It matters only that humans engage in venting their questioning and curiosity-laden minds through the process of searching, and then finding resolution and belief in the answers.

A final word on the subject of Christmas in Butte or at any location: An active involvement in the true heart of Christmas by the faithful is not only a beneficial exercise in humanity, but bodes well for the mind's need for spirituality.

What the mind can imagine, the mind can fulfill,
if not with reality, then with belief.

Jere Murphy, the man and the legend

This piece ends up as a story about Butte's famous chief of police, Jere Murphy, but it didn't start out that way. It was intended as a brief item about warnings and threats I heard around our household when I was little and misbehaving. There were always, "The boogeyman will get you," and "The goblins will carry you off," and in Yiddish, I often heard from my mother, *"A cholerya zol dir chapen."* I always thought this meant, "The devil will get you," but recently, I learned from a teacher of Yiddish that it means, literally, "A cholera will catch you," and in a

general sense, "A plague upon you." Cholera? A disease of epidemic proportions. This from my gentle mother. How severe, but then again, it was a common Yiddish expression of highly exaggerated meaning, maybe something like the one we use today, "Drop dead." And this brings me to Jere Murphy. (What a segue in narration – from a Lithuanian Jewish housewife to an Irish Catholic policeman.) Sometimes my parents or older siblings would say, "Come home early and stay out of trouble, or I'll call Jere Murphy."

Chief Murphy was the dominant authority figure in our small town, a figure I felt personally in my brief encounter with him at the age of 12 when I was arrested for climbing on the side of an apartment building and ended up a frightened kid riding to the jail on Quartz Street seated between the burly Jere and his driver in the famous "Black Maria," a four-door Cadillac convertible.

Now that I've surfaced Jere's name, I'd be remiss in writing about Butte at another time if I failed to explain this man, whose influential and imposing presence was a part of our city awareness, and who gave us a feeling of awe and security – and for some, a twinge of fear.

Jeremiah James Murphy – with his John Wayne-like frame – was a law-and-order man as large as life, an image of a total police force in one courageous man, a man widely respected, a friend to the people and a nemesis of the criminal. He was a 16-year-old Irish immigrant from County Kilkenney who eventually came to Butte where he rose through the ranks of beat policeman to chief of detectives, and finally, to chief of police, a position he held for 24 years. He had the ability to sniff out lawbreakers and get arrests and convictions as if he possessed some super-sense

– almost psychic – which earned him the name of "Jere the Wise," an appellation still remembered.

There are so many dramatic events in the life of Jere Murphy, it is a wonder that Hollywood and writers have not immortalized him as they have Wyatt Earp, Bat Masterson, Pat Garrett, and Wild Bill Hickok. Perhaps someday they will.

But unlike those lawmen, Jere Murphy – although expert with his weapon – was not a gunman. He believed that killing went against God, and would tell his friends, "The Bible says that he who lives by the sword shall perish by the sword." And then he would add: "I don't remember that any exemption is made for peace officers." His gun was in his holster, only to be used as a last resort. Ironically, it was this practice that contributed to his accidental death from a brain concussion three days after his head crashed against a tile floor in a Montana Power Company office while scuffling with a man threatening employees with a pistol.

Though hard on criminals, he was helpful and generous with the needy, disadvantaged, and those ex-cons sincerely trying to make a new life. Typifying Murphy's acts of kindness was his treatment of Shoestring Annie, an impoverished, boisterous street peddler who had had many run-ins with the law and spent brief times in jail. (See page 87.) Learning that Annie was critically ill in her shack near the blighted Cabbage Patch, the chief sent a police car to move her to a hospital, where she died two weeks later. Murphy paid her medical bill out of his own pocket.

He was religious and a family man with two children, but the core of his life was his job; he lived and breathed it as if there were no other mission for him on Earth. Murphy was a towering figure with thick, black hair and mustache, who knew every nook and cranny in Butte, and projected a bearing so threatening and intimidating that lawbreakers during questioning often confessed their guilt rather than face his wrath. His exploits in police work on the local scene – and many involving apprehensions of criminals wanted in other states – were numerous, all of which earned him national recognition as a fearless, tough lawman. It also earned him respect from so-called "big shot" national gang members, who mostly avoided Butte rather than face "Jere the Wise."

In many dangerous situations, he subdued armed men, using his fist instead of a gun, the sort of actions legends are made of. A few cases: Responding to a frantic call from a woman screaming that a man with a gun was threatening people at a roadhouse, Jere sped to the place, and with his gun still in its holster, confronted the gunman with, "Put down that gun!" The man hesitated, and Jere, displaying his massive fist, said, "Put down that gun, or I'll knock your block off with my fist." The man obeyed and went to jail. In facing an assailant, menacingly waving a huge butcher knife, Jere did not need a gun. He flattened the man with a hard right. One of his episodes widely reported in the media was the capture of two dangerous, wanted criminals from the East Coast – Eugene Olson and Donald Van Derve – who were transporting a suitcase containing 28 stolen automatic pistols to the West Coast. They made the mistake of laying-over in Butte. Tipped off about the suitcase by a trainman, Murphy and fellow officer, John Couch, found the two and broke into their hotel room. Van Derve went for his gun, but not in time. Murphy floored him with an uppercut.

A troubling aspect in law enforcement for Jere Murphy and his police force was 14 years of the National Prohibition Act. In a drinking and gambling town like Butte, prohibition was highly unpopular and enforcement was lax. It is said that some members of the Butte police – perhaps even Murphy – accepted payments to tolerate the extensive bootlegging. A legal burden was finally lifted from the duties of both federal and local agents after the repeal of this controversial law in 1933. People of Butte celebrated the event.

Chief Murphy had a fatherly and protective attitude toward Butte, which he referred to as "Our Village." For him, law enforcement and citizen safety were highly personal matters. With his driver, he would cruise Butte streets and alleys in the "Black Maria," searching with his eagle eye for the suspicious and the troublemakers. Sometimes, if someone's behavior didn't seem right, he'd stop the person for questioning, and many times, his suspicions were justified. His uncanny ability to discern the guilty from the innocent and his keen sense in knowing the needy from the hustler were all part of the persona of "Jere the Wise."

The affection and esteem for Jere were evident by the thousands who came to his funeral and the throngs who gathered at St. James Hospital during his final days, wanting to see him and searching for a glimmer of good news. He was eulogized by a Catholic priest who said that, in many aspects, Chief Murphy's acts of charity were Christ-like.

Jere Murphy was a true Irishman from the Old Sod, and it makes one wonder: With so many of the Irish in police work in Butte – either as immigrants or sons of immigrants – is there something in the culture of Ireland that creates a

"Old Sod" sign at Glenbeigh, County Kerry, Ireland.
–photo by J. Sepede

penchant for careers in law enforcement? During and around the time of Jere Murphy, these were some of the Irish peace officers in the Butte area: Tom O'Neill, Ed O'Connor, Jack Duggan, Harry Kinney, Bart Riley, Walter Shay, Jerry Lynch, J.L. Casey, Jim Larkin, Mike Dwyer, John O'Rourke, Jack Quinn, James Mooney, Tim Driscoll, John Couch, James Reynolds, E.W. Wynne, Lou Smith, and Thomas Cody. The Irish around Butte also gravitated toward politics, with many of them becoming mayors and judges.

In the long police career of Jere Murphy, one aspect remains puzzling and lacking in finality: the investigation of the 1917 vigilante murder of Frank Little, a revolutionary labor union activist. (See page 191.) Mayor of Butte, W. H. Maloney, instructed Murphy and several additional deputies to bring Little's killers to justice. Not only is there an enigma of who did it, but also an enigma of why Murphy and his men failed to find the guilty ones. After all, Murphy had a national reputation for his unusual ability to ferret out and arrest lawbreakers, and yet in this case – with six individual trails to six masked vigilantes who lynched Frank Little, and with a witness who saw and heard the men – Murphy and his assistants came up empty and made no arrests. Was it because Murphy was pressured to ignore the case? Why? Was it because at that time Butte's economy, politics, and the press were dominated by the powerful Anaconda Copper Mining Company – certainly a bitter foe of labor union agitators – and was it also because, during a war, many in Butte scorned Little for his anti-government, anti-war activities and were indifferent to the lynching?

One Butte old-timer I spoke with recently said he knew the names of the six vigilantes and that the leader of the group was a former, out-of-favor Butte police officer. The old-timer said nothing further, claiming he was sworn to secrecy. Was this fact or fiction? Someday the true story may emerge.

Regardless of the unsuccessful resolution of the Little case, Murphy's admired stature and his impact on this small, emerging mining town remains a legendary chapter in Montana history.

Some people become prominent because they are present during great challenges, and others rise above the crowd because they are born leaders. They are the best of leaders if they are also decent men. Jere was one of the best of leaders.

Little pieces about Butte

I wonder, do they still unload watermelons from boxcars by tossing them from one person to another? They did in Butte at the Ryan Fruit Co., operated by the Knievel family. Yes, the same clan connected to daredevil Evel Knievel. We kids would patiently watch the melons passed down a line, hoping that one would drop and crack, and in such a case they'd let us have it. Usually we'd come away with a cracked melon; and it was always my belief that one of the kindly grownups dropped a melon on purpose.

* * * *

No reference to the Butte culture would be complete without a mention of a food specialty born in this city in 1920 – the porkchop sandwich. It was created by a Swedish immigrant, John Burkland, who sold it from a small lunch wagon on Mercury Street near Main. The original sandwich, served on a large hamburger bun, contained a bone, but later it was prepared without it. So popular is this item in Butte at present, that just saying "porkchop sandwich" is like saying "Butte." There are two John's porkchop eateries in Butte, but a few other restaurants will also serve this sandwich.

208

* * * *

Elinor Callin. She was in my sixth-grade class at Monroe. I admired her and spoke to her in class, but never socialized with her on a one-on-one basis. She had a nice face with a few freckles and she was an in-between girl: not good looking – not bad looking; not a strong personality – not a weak personality. Just in-between. She was pleasant, nice, and smiled a lot. I could have become fond of her, and through the years, I often think of her and sometimes dream of her. Why?

* * * *

Gus Carkolis was an ambitious kid whose Greek immigrant parents financed him in a little hamburger shop in downtown Butte, which he ran on weekends and after high school. He served hamburgers on small whole-wheat buns with lettuce and pickles – all for a dime. For one week, he lowered the price to a nickel. Even in those days, when food

Gus

was cheap compared to today's prices, I could never figure out how he could sell a hamburger for a nickel. One day I bought three of them. Imagine, only fifteen cents.

* * * *

If I close my eyes, I can see the image clearly: A frosty night...corner of Park and Main at the side of the Rialto Theater...a man with a southern European accent wearing a white apron and grey cap, standing by a steaming copper container selling hot tamales, especially popular during cold weather. The man would wrap a tamale in a sheet of newspaper, and a customer would carry off the warm bundle into the chilly night air. For many years, this man on the corner was a colorful part of Butte's personality and food culture, but it was a competitor, the Italian immigrant brothers – Salvador and Vincent Truzzolino – whose tireless efforts in tamale production and sales eventually established this Butte-made Truzzolino product in national and international markets. Their tamales (originally wrapped in corn husks) were prepared from an old Philippine recipe acquired by Salvador. Isn't it a bit odd? A tamale is a Mexican dish of Spanish origin, but in Butte, they were made in quantity by Italians ever since 1896. Jewish people made them, too. My mother baked the ingredients in a casserole, and it was called tamale pie.

* * * *

I'll never forget my embarrassment when our junkman, old Greetz, caught us kids cheating. We'd find hunks of lead, especially old sink traps, and Greetz would give us three cents a pound for the lead. One time, we had part of a trap and we stuffed rocks and sand in it so that it would weigh more. Greetz discovered our bit of mischief, and we just stood there feeling low. From then on, Greetz never trusted us about anything. Who could blame him?

* * * *

At a Butte High School reunion, at the Copper King Inn, I finally realized why I knew some of my classmates much, much better than others. It was because they were also my classmates for eight years at Monroe Elementary School, thereby making it 12 years around them. I especially remember two, because they were also named Paul. In class, teachers at Monroe would refer to us as the *Three Pauls:* Paul Dosen, Paul Greiner, and Paul Lowney.

* * * *

To this day, when I hear someone give a shrill whistle, a bit of joy floods over me. It's sort of a happy reminder of years ago, that when people whistled at me on streets in Butte, it meant selling a *Montana Standard* tucked under my arm. Selling a paper to make a few coins every Sunday morning meant getting money for college – and it didn't matter if they whistled at me or just hollered "Hey boy – paper!"

* * * *

The small cabin atop a tower about 20 feet high smelled of burning coke from a small heater and from pipe tobacco, but for us kids, this cabin with old Tom in it was a warm and comfortable place to be when the nights were cold and empty. Tom's job was lowering and raising the guard gates for the copper-ore-laden freight cars as the train crossed the intersection of Iron and Main streets. The job was a dreary one for the widower, Tom, sitting alone in the gloom of the night—and because of his solitude, he always welcomed company, and would tell stories about early railroading.

Why should this ordinary experience in this small loft remain so indelible in my mind when, most certainly, other events of greater moment in my young life have faded and vanished? Perhaps a lasting impression came from the eeriness of the room, half lit by an oil lamp, and from the acrid odor of the fire mixed with pipe tobacco smoke; or perhaps it was my sympathetic feeling for the aloneness of Tom, spending night after night in his tiny vigil. The railroad tracks are still there, but the tower and the cabin are gone, and now there is some talk about using the rails to operate a passenger train for a scenic-ride tourist attraction.

212

* * * *

Did we kids in Butte make up some of our own words? Maybe. At least, the dictionary doesn't list a word we constantly used: gah'me. I've never seen it in print, so I'm trying to spell it like it sounds. For us it meant someone who is peculiar, odd, or very funny, like a clown. For instance, in discussing a hilarious character in a movie, we might say, "There was this gah'me guy who...." Webster people, please note.

* * * *

As a place to live, there are many positive points about Butte, but the weather isn't one of them—not unless it's possible to eliminate bitter-cold winters. Obviously, there are many incidents of frozen pipes, frozen cars, frostbitten fingers, and under-heated homes and buildings, but it's the numbers that tell the story. During our family's time in Butte, there was a record cold of 52 degrees below zero, February 9, 1933, and in 1937, there was a wild swing in temperature from 40 degrees above zero on January 15 to 40 degrees below four days later – an 80 degree change – definitely confusing the population in their choice of outdoor clothing.

* * * *

Although hard-cash gambling was tolerated in Butte, I never saw real, money-dispensing slot machines in the city. I did, however, see them in the lobby area of the Gregson Hot Springs complex, some 14 miles west of Butte. We kids played the nickel machine once in awhile, and we had this theory that pulling the handle slowly improved the chances of winning. (I still do that in Nevada.) I doubt if it works, but one of the guys in our group came up with an idea that he said would work. He said that if we stuffed a wad of paper into the end of the coin-dispensing tube, the coins would get caught when someone won. He figured that the player would then leave the machine to find the manager; and at that point, we'd remove the paper and run off with the coins. Well, it worked. A man won with three plums that paid out 12 dimes, and we came away with $1.20. How clever of us! Clever, but wrong. It worked once, but we didn't try it again. I wonder: Would it work in Las Vegas? Probably not. A player wouldn't leave the machine unattended.

* * * *

It was the night we graduated from Butte High School – a time to do something special, so my friend and fellow student, Creighton Carlson, suggested that we walk through the Red Light District in the Mercury Street alley to check out the scantily clad women in the cribs tapping on the windows. Since I had just turned 18, I viewed the women as middle-aged, but in reality, they were probably in their late twenties or early thirties. Their going rate was one dollar, which for me at that time was a lot of money, but not for Creighton, because he had a generous allowance from his mother. After we

Creighton

had walked about halfway through the alley, he stopped, looked at me, and said, "Paul, it's graduation night, and I think it's time you grew up and tasted a little of life and became a man." He handed me a silver dollar. I spent it.

Paul

1939 Chevrolet

"Past" is permanent; "present" is transient

At that time, the 1939 Chevrolet appeared so modern – if not futuristic – that years later, in retrospect, I recalled my original impressionable feelings about this automobile and I began wondering about all worldly items that are new but born of the old; and about the philosophy of progress and change; and about how past, present, and future all string together in the same infinite spool.

The Chevrolet was parked on West Broadway Street in Butte. When I saw it, I thought: *This is it. This is the ultimate in modern. How can any car ever become more up-to-date, more advanced? This is the terminal in the evolution of automotive technology—this sleek, streamlined car with wrap-around fenders and the latest in suspension, roadability, and combustion engineering.*

How wrong I was—just as wrong as a congressman years ago who proposed saving money by closing the U.S. Patent Office because, in his opinion, everything was already invented. Certainly, the Lexus, the Corvette, the Mercedes, the Jaguar, the Porsche, and a few others look as good as it gets, both visually and mechanically, but who's to say how these present vehicles will compare when matched against those in the year 2500 or 3000? Perhaps in future years, these machines will be fusion-powered and travel in the air and on water as well as on the ground.

Makes one wonder: *In a backward view from the distant future, we at present are ancients and all our works are antiquities.*

Throughout history, those in previous civilizations believed that their present was the newest and the best and the pinnacle of progress. The Romans must have felt that way when they built the aqueducts, and the ancients when they first forged copper and then iron; and when the loom was invented; and years before, when the Phoenicians devised the alphabet; and more recently, how advanced people felt when the human voice was first transmitted from one continent to another. And now we enter what appears to be the ultimate: the exploration of outer space, nanotechnology, the literature of the human genome, cloning, and the secrets of how our bodily atoms function.

All of these advances move endlessly on the pathways of progress and change, and will continue to do so just as long as the human brain yearns to know more and more and strives with insatiable hunger to explore the unknown and to replace the mysteries of life and the universe with the scientific facts of life and the universe.

When, today, I witness something totally new and astounding, as I did with the 1939 Chevrolet, I marvel at it, but a part of me wonders if this, too, like the image from a lantern slide, will shine brightly only for a moment and then yield to its transient nature.

Just as our physical world is ever-changing, so, too, is our sociological world. The "now" fashions and styles; the hip, pop, and cool tend to mock the past as old-fashioned and banal, failing to realize that in time, the "now" also becomes old-fashioned and banal.

As we move from past to present to future, what then is a basic ideal in our sociological world that is unchanging and timeless? It is this: *Achieving a goodness of the human spirit that enriches all life it touches.*

*In a backward view from the distant future,
we at present are ancients and all our works
are antiquities.*

A boy's journey to the humane movement

"The question is, not can they reason, and not can they talk, but can they suffer?"
– Jeremy Bentham, English philosopher

This piece is a departure from my usual recitation of events in my life in Butte. Even though the setting is Butte, most of the following words are an essay on the ethics in the human/animal relationship. The story begins with my boyish adventures in killing small, defenseless creatures for the fun of it, and then segues to my acceptance and my advocacy of what the great humanitarian, Albert Schweitzer, calls "reverence for life." If the humane movement is of little interest to some of you readers, then you may skip the essay part – but I hope you don't.

During my teens in Butte, two events stirred my emotions and engaged my reason, and eventually led me to embrace the animal-humane movement. Before the age of nine, I was shooting a gun, albeit only a single-shot, BB air rifle, but it was my own gun, and unfortunately, I used it destructively. I was a good shot, and it was easy for me to hit a sparrow sitting on the edge of a roof or on a telephone wire or in a tree. I thought nothing of it. To me, sparrows had no feelings, and besides that, it was what my gun was all about – to shoot things.

But it wasn't regret over killing sparrows that brought

me to the humane movement, nor was it any advice or guidance from my parents or other adults. It was my own insight from two events.

Event one: I was fly-fishing for trout in the Big Hole River, some 30 miles south of Butte. I didn't particularly like fishing, but the grownups did it, and fishing was always a big topic of conversation. My older brother, Sam, took me along and then wandered off downstream. I found a beaver dam, and using a Royal Coachman lure, I cast my line toward the center of the pooled-up water. The fish must have been hungry, because I easily caught three of them. It bothered me to watch the fish gasping and wiggling around trying to get back into the water where there was life-giving oxygen. I sometimes saw the grownups knock the fish's head against a rock to end the wiggling, and so that's what I did, too.

But this wasn't the end of my fishing event. That night I had a vivid dream. In my dream, I pulled the hook from the trout's mouth, and the fish said, "Ouch, you're hurting me," and then it looked at me sadly, perhaps knowing death was near, and a large tear from one eye rolled down its scaly head.

I never forgot that dream and I never fished again. I realize that this experience was an emotional one and perhaps an overkill in empathy, but it was a feeling that possessed me and stayed with me the rest of my life. Yes, I do eat fish, and I'm grateful for their flesh to help sustain my life, but I do so with a sense that I am caught up in the natural laws of survival and the food chain, and it eases my mind a bit to know that the fish I eat are not innocent vegetarians – they are killers that eat fish just as I eat fish.

But at my hand, I will not take their lives, unless to save mine. Let me add that I see a clear difference between the sport fishermen and the commercial fishermen. Even though they eat the fish, the sport fishermen enjoy the game and the recreation of catching and killing fish – and with a different goal, commercial fishermen are part of the serious business of survival, and like a farmer, simply reap the harvest to provide food. Also, there is the same comparison with the game hunter and the butcher. The moral differences are a matter of value and attitude. Life is precious and miraculous. There must be something more noble in the human spirit than enjoying or finding recreation in killing living things.

My fishing experience started me thinking about taking the lives of creatures for sport, but it was my second adventure with killing that brought me totally and irrecoverably into the animal-humane movement.

Event two: I was 12 when I first owned a .22 caliber, bolt action rifle. My brother, Hank, had one, too. I remember one day as vividly as yesterday. Hank and I were on the outskirts of Butte beyond the copper-mine slag dumps in an area called the "Diggings," which was flat, dry, and covered with sagebrush and tumbleweeds. Gophers were scampering about – dozens of them running from one hole to another. Maybe there was a reason for this outpouring of gophers, but all I thought of at the time was the great opportunity for target shooting. With the experience I had with my BB gun, I was able to hit gophers on the run. Most of those I shot would kick for a while and then lie still. What a bloodbath! But to me, it was target practice – just animals with no feelings.

Then it happened. I hit one gopher with a glancing blow, and the bullet tore the flesh off its side and I could see its ribs. It dove down a hole, still alive. I remember hearing the thud of the bullet hitting its body and I wondered if the impact of a bullet makes the same mushy thud when it hits a human. And like my experience with the fish, the thought of killing bothered me. In sort of a grim, humorous way, I visualized that gopher with its side torn off, crawling down the hole, bleeding and dying, while other gophers, probably his family, gathered about wondering how to help the mortally wounded relative. At that moment, I transferred my emotions from one life-form to another life-form, realizing that the bullet impact, the mortal wound, and the dying would be the same for a human; and when I made this connection in my youthful mind, this empathy was to remain with me. I put away my .22 rifle, and from then on, I never killed another animal, large or small.

These two experiences – my vivid dream of the trout and the slaughtering of gophers – started me thinking about all the animals everywhere – both in the wild and in the human community.

In the wild, animals must survive and rear their young in the harsh environment of raw nature. For the animals preyed upon, there's constant danger of a brutal death; and for the predators, it's "kill or starve": a snake swallows a live creature; the lion tears out the throat of a terrified wildebeest; wolves devour a newborn fawn.

As cruel as animals are to one another, they do so in abeyance to their evolved genetic code. They do not make moral judgments or ethical decisions. But humans do. Therefore, when we bring animals into the human community as our charges, we are obliged morally and ethically to care for them and to use compassion and empathy to lessen their suffering. Animals are riddled throughout our society, and we are involved with them, but unfortunately, in present times, we are still influenced by traditional stereotypes about animals that have changed little during the passing years; and we accept as normal and commonplace some of the painful practices used for centuries on these speechless creatures.

If I've learned anything at all from my years in the humane movement, it's this: Many good and kindly people with compassion unwittingly help along animal cruelty, not realizing that with their support, they subsidize needless activities that cause pain – activities such as circuses, rodeos, dog races, cramped and inadequate zoos; using products obtained by steel trapping; and consuming the flesh of certain classes of animals raised and slaughtered under barbaric conditions.

The human-inflicted suffering upon animals is widespread, often justified by the specious religious notion that animals were put here for our benefit, when in fact, animals were here millions and millions of years before humans came along and subdued them with higher brain function.

Humans are carnivores, but they are also plant eaters, so a question arises: Is it necessary for humans to kill for food? Probably, in arctic and desert lands incapable of yielding plant food; but in crop-raising countries, humans, if they chose, could exist by eating soil-grown foods.

In his book, *The Prophet*, Kahlil Gibran, beautifully describes his empathy for animals killed for food:

"...Would that you could live on the fragrance of the earth, and like an air plant be sustained by light. But since you must kill to eat...let it then be an act of worship. And let your board stand an altar on which the pure and innocent of forest and plain are sacrificed for that which is purer and still more innocent in man. When you kill a beast say to him in your heart, 'By the same power that slays you, I too am slain; and too shall be consumed. For the law that delivered you into my hand shall deliver me into a mightier hand. Your blood and my blood is naught but the sap that feeds the tree of heaven.'..."

The animals we eat are the innocent ones – not killers, but vegetarians. If one suffers guilt from eating animals, there is this logical but impractical, tongue-in-cheek advice on how to feel less guilt: Use *The Law of Just Compensation*. Eat only the animals that are killers, such as lions, tigers, coyotes, weasels, owls, snakes, and alligators.

In the production of food from animals, the suffering and privation is monumental, when one considers some of the cruel practices in the factory farm systems. I won't enumerate the painful details here, but they are clearly spelled out in the publications issued by a score of humane societies, especially by People for Ethical Treatment of Animals (PETA).

In what I hope is a reasonable and ethical note about the pain and suffering of animals used for medical, pharmaceutical, and industrial research, I offer these observations: The common rationale is: The research and experimentation is justified on the basis of saving and enhancing human lives. This very point poses a dilemma for anyone seeking an ethical definition in the human/animal relationship. The dilemma is "animal lives versus human lives" and "animal suffering versus human benefits."

At the outset, I suggest that if it is absolutely essential that animals be used for research and experimentation, we must use every means possible to reduce pain and privation; and above all, we should admit that the suffering we cause animals is wrong, just as wrong as if some super-advanced life-form on planet Kleon used humans for experimentation and justified it by saying, "But it saves Kleon lives." The moral point comes down to this: When we find it necessary for our own survival to cause suffering for animals, we should acknowledge – if only philosophically – that what we do is unethical and that it is simply a matter of the false historical dictum: "Might makes right." Just be grateful if you don't come back in another life as an animal in a research laboratory.

As a footnote to this subject, there is a group of medical doctors actively opposed to "cruel and painful animal experiments." The organization is called Physicians Committee for Responsible Medicine (PCRM). They point out alternate non-animal methods for research and experimentation.

A serious stumbling block to the humane movement is the mindset held by many good people that animals are "things" or "objects" devoid of feelings. I saw proof of this attitude in my own childhood in Butte. My mother was a kindly, compassionate woman who became emotional when she saw a drop of blood oozing from a scratch on my finger. Yet, to conform to kosher killing, she would allow a chicken to lie around the backyard in a gunny sack with its feet tied with string – lying there in its own waste for perhaps an hour or two awaiting the handyman to come and slit its throat. Obviously, my mother didn't feel compassion or guilt over the pain or suffering of that pitiful creature. She was just doing the customary – what her mother in the Old

Country did. It was just a non-feeling chicken for the Sunday dinner.

The point of the chicken story is this: Too often we are guilty of repeating tradition and custom without question. It's time to re-examine our cultural stereotyped thinking about the suffering and pain inherent in the human/animal relationship.

For those who justify the ill treatment of animals on the premise that animals have no soul, consider this: Soul is a theory, but pain is real. A moral quandary could arise from research now in progress at the Gorilla Foundation at Woodside, California. Using sign language, a female gorilla, Koko, has learned the meanings of more than 1,000 words and has an IQ of around 82. What if Koko were taught religion and baptized a Christian? A point to consider: There is less than a two-percent difference in the genetic codes of humans and apes. As zoologist Jane Goodall observed: "The border between human and animal is very blurred."

Through humane organizations, I have become aware of the many specific details of human-committed animal cruelty, and I am often surprised by how little the general public is aware of these details. Perhaps the comparison is unfair, but I sometimes feel that the attitude of many people, indifferent to the plight of animals in factory farms, slaughter houses, and research labs, parallels the claims made after World War II by Germans living near concentration camps when they protested with contriteness, "But we didn't know what was going on in there." One might resent the comparison by saying, "You can't compare people with animals. After all, they are only animals." This thinking poses one of the difficulties in building support for the humane movement: "They are only animals." An appropriate response to this point is the words of a leading English philosopher, Jeremy Bentham: *The question is, not can they reason, and not can they talk, but can they suffer?*

The references humans make about the animal lives they terminate are couched in euphemisms, as if these softer terms are less troubling to the conscience and a sense of guilt. For instance, it's not a hunk of blood-soaked animal corpse we are eating. It's prime rib au jus. It isn't the decapitated head of an elk or moose hanging in the den. It's a trophy. It isn't the slain carcass of a doe that a hunter ties to his van. It's game. We don't kill unwanted or suffering cats and dogs. We put them to sleep. We don't slaughter seals. We harvest them.

What will the future bring in the human/animal relationship? In time, there will be a responsive awareness of the pain we cause these creatures, but the awareness will move slowly, since we primarily think in terms of relieving human suffering, and this is understandable. We will have more regard and empathy for animals when we finally realize that animals are in the same family as humans, lacking only in higher brain function, but nevertheless possessing the ability to love, to nurture, to feel depression and loneliness, and most certainly, to feel mental and physical pain. The work to be done is:

1. Activate an educational program at the school level informing young minds of animal suffering, and creating awareness of how much of this suffering is caused by humans. Also, a similar message should be brought to the adult community via subsidized and free outlets in the media.
2. Increase the effectiveness of political-action groups and lobbies to work with government legislative bodies to bring about much-needed humane legislation.
3. Greatly increase funding through both public and private finance to enlarge and broaden support for those groups engaged in lessening or eliminating the needless suffering of those animals within reach of the human community.

Also, it would be helpful for the many splinter animal groups to merge into fewer, but more powerful, well-funded organizations to carry out educational, legislative, and service programs.

I've always hoped that philanthropists would donate as much money to the humane movement as they do to symphony orchestras and other humanities. On my personal wish list: I wish I were a billionaire so I could donate multimillions to put such humane programs in place. (Billionaires, please note.)

A prophecy: With sufficient funds and with efforts by the compassionate and the energetic, there will be at long last the dawning of a new age in our relationship with animals in which empathy and compassion rule. It will not happen in my lifetime, and perhaps not in my grand-children's lifetime, but consider that, from a geological standpoint, civilization is still infant and still evolving, and that the truly civilized, with the gift of reason and conscience, will eventually act in consensus to ease the widespread suffering of creatures under our domain.

It is fitting to close this essay with the words of Albert Schweitzer, the world-famous humanitarian, philosopher, physician, theologian, and musician: *Until he extends the circle of his compassion to all living things, man will not, himself, find peace.*

If we begin with empathy, our painful treatment of lesser creatures will diminish.

"The greatness of a nation and its moral progress can be judged by the way its animals are treated...the more helpless a creature, the more entitled it is to protection by man from the cruelty of man."

Mahatma Gandhi

Some funny things happened in Butte
Laughter has no foreign accent.

For the amusement of some of my friends, I sometimes pretend to be a stand-up comedian and I rattle off several stories and quips about happenings in Butte, Montana. Many of the items are original, a few are partially true, and others are simply stored in my memory from sources I know not where.

One person who likes my routine is Jimmy, the young boyfriend of one of my part-time employees. He'd say, "Do the Montana jokes," and finally, one day he said, "Why don't you put them in your Montana book?" At the time, I rejected the idea because this present book (unlike my previous books of humor) is rather serious and autobiographical.

But what if I put these light-hearted, mostly fictitious bits at the end of the book, just as dessert comes at the end of a more substantial offering? Good idea.

Ergo: That's what I'm doing. So, Jimmy, here goes.

* * * *

I was born on a Great Northern train crossing the Continental Divide about 12 miles from Butte. My birth caused a loud shouting argument. The conductor wanted to charge half-fare for me, and my father refused to pay. Sometimes people ask me what sign I was born under and I tell them: IN CASE OF EMERGENCY, PULL THE RED HANDLE.

* * * *

Butte is a mile above sea level, and the air is very thin. Let me explain. When I was little, I entered a contest, "Why I Use Ivory Soap." I wrote in and said, "I use Ivory soap because I'm dirty." I won a football, but I couldn't blow it up. There was hardly enough air for me.

* * * *

What I remember mostly about my life in Butte was that we were very poor. On my birthday, my mother would show me a picture of a cake. One time, burglars broke into our small, miserable basement flat on South Wyoming Street, and, as I recall, they didn't take things – they left things. I remember one time our landlord, Scotty Fries (who was also principal of Butte High School) came to collect $30 for a month's rent and my mother said to him, "What about the floor?" and Scotty said, "What about it?" My mother said, "We'd like to have one."

* * * *

I think there were too many to feed in our household. I got this feeling because my parents would wrap my school lunch in a travel folder, and sometimes, when I'd come home from school, I'd find out they had moved, and they'd never pin a note to the door to say where.

* * * *

One weekend, my friend Raymond and I went overnight hiking in Maude S. Canyon, located in the mountainous Continental Divide. We decided to hike into the rugged V Canyon, and we became hopelessly lost for three days. Fortunately, we were able to survive on roots and berries, and we finally found our way out. The unkindest cut of all was when I came home and learned that my parents didn't miss me until the second day, and then they sprang into action. They sold my bicycle.

Oddly enough, something similar happened at our Boy Scout camp at Ruby Creek. Again, Raymond and I became lost – this time after wandering off during a supervised 14-mile hike. When we finally got back to camp, we heard that when we hadn't answered morning roll call, the camp director acted with great dispatch. He called the mess hall and said: "There'll be two less for breakfast – possibly lunch and dinner, too."

* * * *

Jack Prather played flute with the Butte High School orchestra, and always told us his ambition was to solo. Finally, he got his chance. He was chosen to play a solo part in the *Intermezzo* from Bizet's *Carmen Suite*. It turned out to be a disaster. Two fruit flies landed on his score and he played them for quarter notes.

* * * *

Benny Crowley was the only one in our band of small kids who smoked, but only when he could steal cigarettes from his older brother, Jimmy, or when he managed to find some Bull Durham and roll his own with rice papers. When he didn't have either, he'd smoke tea or coffee or the rust-colored dry seeds we called Indian tobacco that appeared on weeds growing near the copper-mine slag dumps. On one occasion, he rolled a cigarette using crushed cornflakes. We asked how he liked the cornflakes, and he said, "Fine, except once in a while I wake up in the middle of the night craving milk and sugar."

* * * *

The guys in our gang at Monroe Elementary School considered anyone a girl who would use indoor plumbing to do number one – especially when there was a perfectly good alley directly across the street. It was probably from our school that the well-known expression arose: "Don't eat the yellow snow."

* * * *

Our class comedian at Butte High School was Rune. Examples: When Bobby Doull complained that Swede Dahlberg, the coach, wouldn't let him go out for football because he didn't weigh enough, Rune said to Bobby, "If you drink a lot of water, you'll weigh more on the scales."

Bobby insisted he could hold only so much water, and Rune said he could hold more. "How?" Bobby asked. With a straight face, Rune said, "Eat a sponge." …The teacher was drilling us in geographical spellings. She looked at Rune and said, "Spell Mississippi." Rune hesitated for a moment and then said, "Do you mean the river or the state?"

* * * *

As a child, I was precocious and resented being treated like a child, even though I was one. Well, I'd show them. At the age of five, I remember two incidents. In the Butte Library, one of the librarians approached me and said, "Hi, little man, want a copy of *Goldilocks and the Three Bears?*, or maybe you'd like to see *Little Red Riding Hood*." I fixed my cold, green eyes on her and said, "Please hoist me up to the card index file. I'm looking for Immanuel Kant's *Critique of Pure Reason* – the German-language edition." That was the last time she ever mistook me for a child.

It was the same year. I was in our front yard on South Main Street, looking intently at a dandelion in a patch of flowers. A passerby, a tailor named Henry Pissott, smiled at me and said, "Sonny, are you enjoying the pretty flowers?" I gave him my special aloof stare and said, "I have a cursory interest in botany. At the moment, I am relating empirical criteria to the hypothesis, 'Weeds will inherit the Earth.'" At any age, I never could stand condescension.

* * * *

Butte's busiest junkman was old Martin Greetz who had a reputation for being the meanest man in town. Nobody actually saw him doing anything mean, so probably this came from his defensive, unfriendly attitude; and this attitude was undoubtedly a reflection of the way people treated him, because he was such an unsavory-looking character with old, ragged, smelly clothes and a sneering face etched with deep wrinkles like grooves in an old-fashioned washboard – and when he spoke, you could see his crooked, brown-stained teeth.

He always carried a deep leather purse that was more like a sock. I can still see him reaching deep into this purse to find a few coins to pay us kids for pieces of metal we'd bring him, mostly scraps of lead and hunks of copper wire with the insulation removed.

There were some stories going around about old Greetz. Someone said that when he read *Uncle Tom's Cabin*, he thought Simon Legree was the hero. One of our town jokesters started the rumor that Greetz kept mice in his woodshed and that he was training them to kill cats. Though they couldn't prove it, one person claimed Greetz sent calendars to lifers in the penitentiary at Deer Lodge, and still another person said he wrote RX on Christian Science reading room windows.

Greetz had a lot of money, but lived a stingy life in a small, dirty cabin on his junkyard lot; and he still had the first nickel he ever made, and this was *literally* true, because the nickel was counterfeit.

* * * *

I wanted a cat, but my parents said they were too poor to feed one, so I found a big, black beetle and attached it to a string, and it became my cat. I called it Sher Khan, the name of the tiger in Kipling's *The Jungle Book*, and I took it everywhere with me. One day, some big kids teased me about Sher Khan, so I said to it – kill!, and then one of the guys stepped on my cat.

* * * *

Alfie Dawson was known as Butte High School's most talented graphic artist. After he graduated, he went into sculpting. He collected bottles, bottle caps, bits of glass, scrap wire, tinfoil, tin cans, hunks of bark, lollipop sticks, and shiny stones. In five years, he managed to finish his creation – a 12-foot-high pile of junk.

* * * *

During my early years in Butte, super-giant firecrackers were legal for the Fourth of July. In our gang, we'd consider anyone a sissy who'd light these giants and then run away while the fuse was burning. We'd hold the firecrackers in our bare hands. I remember the old gang. There were

Stumpy, No Hands, Lefty, Two Fingers, and Three Fingers.
Those were the girls. *Three Fingers* later became a thief.
All she'd ever steal were bowling balls.

* * * *

For the Fourth, some of the bigger kids – Frenchy, Babe,
and Rags – wanted an explosion loud enough to wake the
whole city, so they found some dynamite and caps at an
abandoned copper mine, and at dawn they took the explo-
sives to the Hebgen Park baseball field. They rigged them
for firing, but something went horribly wrong and the dynamite
blew Frenchy, Babe, and Rags all over the field. One of the
cops investigating the tragedy, Eddie O'Malley, had played
baseball with Frenchy and remarked that in his experience,
it was the first time Frenchy ever made it to third base.

* * * *

After a Butte High basketball game, a few of us went to
the Nanking Restaurant on South Main Street. I ordered my
usual – chicken-tomato chow mein with pea pods. After I
paid my bill, the cashier asked me how I liked my food, and
I said, "The chow mein was fine, but I didn't care for the
fortune in my cookie, and I don't deserve a bad fortune."
She said, "Don't worry, bad fortunes don't come true – only
good fortunes come true," and then she asked, "What was
the fortune?" I read it: "Soon you will cross great waters,"

and then I added, "Crossing great waters can mean crossing the big divide – dying." She said, "No, that's not what it means. It probably means an ocean trip. Here, let me give you another cookie." I broke it open and the fortune read: "You are troubled. Please disregard previous cookie."

* * * *

One of the students who stood out at Butte High School was Leo Lippman, the milkman. He was in his mid-30s, Jewish, came from Europe as a small child, and had a strong desire to finally get a high school diploma. Besides arising at dawn to deliver milk and attend a full schedule of classes, he had an evening busing job at the Chequamegon Restaurant. Somehow, Leo found time to do his homework and was a top student. Often in class he looked worn and ragged, prompting one wise guy to remark, "Leo looks like a shell of his former self. I'll bet if you put him to your ear, you could hear the ocean."

* * * *

At Monroe Elementary School, the guys called him "Blindy" because his glasses were really thick – like the bottom of a Coke bottle. If the sun was shining, the teacher wouldn't let him go outside at recess because he started fires.

* * * *

I was with my two brothers at Butte's man-made recreational Lake Avoca (no longer exists). At that time, I couldn't swim and I fell out of a canoe and into the lake. My brothers rescued me and brought me ashore. They tried giving me artificial respiration, but I kept getting up and running away.

– the end –